Mother Teresa:
Her People and her Work

Desmond Doig was the first journalist ever to
write about Mother Teresa, when she had just
left the security of a rich Order for the poverty of
the streets of Calcutta, and he had just started
writing for *The Statesman,* India's leading newspaper. This book is based on the many articles
Mr. Doig has written about Mother Teresa in the
succeeding twenty-seven years, arising from the
unique experience he has gained by his deep
friendship with her and knowledge of her work.

Raghu Rai is also a long-standing friend of
Mother Teresa and accompanied her when she
visited Bangladesh. He is a photographer of high
international repute.

Desmond Doig

Mother Teresa

Her People and Her Work

Collins
Fount Paperbacks

First published in Great Britain by
William Collins Sons & Co Ltd, Glasgow, 1976

First issued in Fount Paperbacks, 1978
This edition first published by
Fount Paperbacks, 1978
Second Impression June 1980

Made and printed in Great Britain by
William Collins Sons & Co Ltd, Glasgow

For my Mother who,
while the Raj looked askance
and with the little she had,
nursed and tended the poor.

Contents

List of Illustrations

Lord, make me an instrument of Your peace,
Where there is hatred, let me sow love;
Where there is injury, pardon;
Where there is doubt, faith;
Where there is despair, hope;
Where there is darkness, light;
And where there is sadness, joy.
O divine Master, grant that I may not
So much seek to be consoled as to console;
To be understood as to understand;
To be loved as to love;
For it is in giving that we receive;
It is in pardoning that we are pardoned;
And it is in dying
That we are born to eternal life.

St Francis of Assisi

PRIME MINISTER

FOREWORD

How appropriate that this book should begin with
St. Francis' beautiful and well-loved prayer. For it
so eloquently epitomises the gentleness, the love and
the compassion that radiate from Mother Teresa's tiny
person.

Who else in this wide world reaches out to the
friendless and the needy so naturally, so simply, so
effectively? Tagore wrote "there rest Thy feet where
live the poorest, and lowliest, and lost". That is
where Mother Teresa is to be found - with no thought
of, or slightest discrimination between colour or
creed, language or country.

She lives the truth that prayer is devotion,
prayer is service. Service is her concern, her religion,
her redemption. To meet her is to feel utterly humble,
to sense the power of tenderness, the strength of love.

(Indira Gandhi)

New Delhi,
September 26, 1975.

Prologue

When Mother Teresa first learnt that yet another book was being written about her, she very characteristically thought for a while, then requested that it be about her people and her work, and not about personalities. Mother's people are the poorest of the poor, be they in India, where her work began, or in the affluent countries of the world to where it has spread. Her work, shared by a growing number of Missionaries of Charity, is to give help and love where it is needed. The Brothers and Sisters of the Order are today working in the ghettos of New York, the slums of London, in Australia, South America and in the shadow of the Vatican at the Pope's personal request. Mother Teresa maintains that the suffering of the poor in affluent countries is more a searing loneliness and rejection. In India, strong bonds of family, religion and tradition lessen the rigours of poverty, but it is still there, a product of history, geography and exploding population.

This book in trying to be true to Mother Teresa's request concerns itself with poverty that might appear to be out of all proportion to the many achievements and attractions of a great, emerging country like India. It also concerns itself innocently with personalities, despite Mother Teresa's expressed wishes, because the extraordinary work described is inevitably the endeavour of a comparatively few people, however much they might be carrying out the will of God. Without Mother Teresa, there would have been no Missionaries of Charity, just as without Calcutta there would have been no Mother Teresa.

Calcutta, a city I love, has had its problems ever since it began. The Calcutta of this book is not the city of millionaire merchants and thriving commercial houses, neither is it peopled by men of letters, politicians, artists and businessmen. It is the city of the poor and Mother Teresa. One could not have been without the other.

Whilst writing this book we have talked to a number of people, such as Father Henry and Sister Agnes, who have known Mother Teresa for many years. Inevitably their accounts overlap in places, but because each has a personal story to tell and a slightly different slant on Mother Teresa we have decided not to cut passages which to some people may seem a repetition but to us appear more like variations on a theme.

One other explanation is necessary. The 'we' I have used so commonly in the book is not the royal 'we'. It encompasses several people. Raghu Rai, Teki and Kalyan Singh, who took the photographs, while Dubby Bhagat and I made notes and wielded tape-recorders. Raghu Rai, an internationally-known photographer of enormous sensitivity, is an old friend of Mother Teresa and admits to having been inspired by her into taking some of his best photographs. We thank Mother Teresa and her Missionaries of Charity for not only putting up with us but making us feel a part of their Congregation. We also thank Father Henry and Michael Gomes for being patient and helping so much.

Then there are Krishna Kumar Jaiswal and Padma Vaswani who persevered with many badly recorded tapes and our spidery first drafts; Dhun Batlivala, my long-suffering secretary, who also unravelled tapes and typed several 'final' manuscripts; friends and colleagues Sadhan Banerjee and Michael Chering who read, corrected and advised; artist friend and colleague Ratan Pradhan, who helped make a difficult selection from hundreds of brilliant photographs, aided by Bimal Sen; and Lolita and Aditya Nehru and Rajat Bose who listened patiently and advised. I cannot thank them enough.

Finally, there is my good friend Dubby Bhagat, who helped and encouraged every slum, Home for the suffering, comma and full-stop of the way. By taking down the first draft in laborious longhand, he almost wrote the book. He deservingly takes the last bow.

1. Shantinagar: A Place for Peace

Calcutta, always teeming with people, was almost asleep when we called on Mother Teresa at 5 a.m. It was one of those flat, grey, pre-monsoon mornings when the pot-holed streets, the peeling buildings and the crippled trees of the city merged one with the other so that one hardly noticed at first the sleeping bodies along the pavements. They lay in haphazard rows like corpses awaiting burial, covered with taut, dirty sheets, or rags, or paper, or nothing at all. Here and there was grudging movement around small fires from which smoke lifted then hung like a grey canopy over the sleepers. Women cooked frugal morning meals while naked children awoke and swarmed about, and street dogs that detached themselves from the sleeping figures stretched and edged hungrily towards the warmth and the smell of food. The first tram-cars rattled noisily through the empty streets, dilapidated monsters that just hours later would be festooned with people on their way to work.

In Lower Circular Road, one of the city's main arteries, where affluent city merchants once lived in garden palaces, it was crow-complaining time, a sound so typically Calcutta. Past an all-night Muslim eating-house, close by a mosque pearly with porcelain mosaic and beyond a still shuttered 'thieves' bazaar now respectable with second- and third-hand dealers, and almost below the twin spires of St James's Protestant Church, is the Mother House of the Missionaries of Charity. Entrance is down a narrow cul-de-sac, through an unpretentious black door that opens to the pulling of a chain, hung close by a board that reads, 'Mother M. Teresa MC'. More usually than not, someone has forgotten to adjust the little shutter that proclaims 'In' or 'Out'. It hardly matters. To thousands of Calcutta's destitute and needy the opening of that door means help of some kind.

Ours, too, was a selfish request. We were there to take Mother Teresa with us to her leper colony at Shantinagar some two hundred miles and four hours away by train, which meant that we would be keeping her away from her people in Calcutta a whole day. She had told us just days before that while we, ruthlessly interviewing and photographing her, were also doing God's work, for her the time spent with the likes of us was a personal sacrifice because it kept her from the needs of her people, the poorest of the poor.

We pulled the bell and heard its metallic summons overpowered by the clatter of bolts being drawn and there was a jovial Sister peering at us. We were obviously the day's first needy. Hesitation. Would we please wait in the tiny courtyard? Mother would be with us in a minute. The door to the familiar parlour was closed, but one leading to an inner courtyard was open and through it we could see Sisters in their white saris fleeting soundlessly about their chores. The day had quickened, and a sulphurous glow that lit a grotto in the courtyard seemed to give substance to the swell of chanting voices from a chapel upstairs. They sang like angels. A cliché, perhaps, but no other description fits.

Quite suddenly there was Mother surrounded by a chatter of nuns. Small. Faded pink, well scrubbed. Blue

eyes. A character of wrinkles. 'Am I late, eh?' she said,
bustling us through the front door and into the lane.
I am always surprised by her smallness, and I've known
her for years. My early photographs of her reassure me
that she has hardly changed : more urgent, more tired,
more deeply lined, perhaps, but still dynamic, still strong,
still determined – always wondrously compassionate. Her
smile is a benediction.

Though Mother Teresa now travels all about India
and the world, and ventures into the slums of Calcutta
which can be a far more harrowing experience, her
settings out are each marked with surprising farewell.
Now, as we waited for her beside the car, some eight
of her Sisters formed themselves into a group whose good
cheer didn't hide their anxiety. They were obviously
loath to let Mother go : one could almost touch the bond
between them. 'Bye-bye, Mother', 'God bless you,
Mother', 'Mother, come back soon', 'Look after yourself, Mother' and a mumble of other half-fears tenderly
expressed. Inside the car as it began to move, Mother
leaned forward and called out a 'God bless you'. A fleeting look of anxiety, of which I am sure she was un-
aware, seemed to suggest that she, too, was reluctant
to leave. She confided afterwards that when she had
made this date with us she had forgotten that it was
the day on which several of her newly-ordained nuns
were leaving the Mother House for far-flung centres of
the Missionaries of Charity in India. When I suggested
we might call off the visit, Mother said one of those firm
noes with which there is no argument, but asked if it
would be all right if we took an earlier train back. If
we could, she might at least see off the batches going
to South India and Darjeeling.

For Mother Darjeeling, in the Himalayan foothills,

must hold a very special place, for it was there she went as a young Yugoslav Loreto nun just arrived from Loreto Abbey, Rathfarnham, in Dublin. And it was on a train to Darjeeling many years later that she heard God's call to leave the Loreto Order and set out alone to work among the poorest of India's poor.

As we drove through the labyrinth of streets now clamorously awakening to a new day, Mother looked with great feeling upon the huddles of still sleeping bodies and remarked to the young Sister accompanying her, 'There are so many, eh? There seem to be more than usual.'

By the time we got to Howrah Station, which on this particular day appeared more burdened with homeless, hungry people who slept everywhere, on the platforms, on parapets, and even on the busy road so that it seemed we might crush them, it was easy to understand Mother's passion to gather them all up, to help them, to give them love. Her serene face looked strained and her hands were tightly clasped about her rosary. Here, in one place, was a shattering glimpse of what Mother Teresa is all about : a single frail woman in a white sari reaching out to a multitude of homeless and bewildered, nameless and destitute, diseased and dying people.

'We've set up a small centre at the station,' Mother explained. 'The Sisters and Brothers are doing excellent work.' That again is Mother Teresa, never sentimental, never maudlin, but invariably practical and down-to-earth, qualities that have prevented her from being submerged even as she set out alone to take upon herself the burden of Calcutta's deprived.

'*Mataji, Mataji!*' (Mother, Mother) called a porter running towards the car. 'Is it the Coalfield Express then?' Mother spoke to him fluently in Hindi as we moved through the dense crowd on the platform. She and the young Sister carried coarse cloth bags; the porter had insisted on carrying the meagre roll of bedding which belonged to the young Sister who would be staying at Shantinagar. It suddenly struck me to ask Mother how we would travel : she with us by first class, or we with her in a crowded general compartment. 'We have a second-class railway pass,' she said, and I remembered how this darling nun had once offered to work her passage as an air hostess. I suddenly and ludicrously wondered if she would have donned a rustle of patterned Indian silk, the uniform of air hostesses.

The porter had dumped the luggage where a general compartment would draw up when the train steamed in. I was in a fair state of anguish wondering whether my friends and I should follow Mother meekly into the claustrophobic crush of a second-class Indian railway compartment, and that on a hot summer's day, or whether I should, I thought heretically, persuade her to share the comparative luxury of the first-class compartment with us. My devils won. 'Mother,' I said, 'it's going to be very hot and dusty. Why don't you travel with us?'

'If you like,' she said casually. And even as the train steamed in we rushed off to up-grade the tickets. It was only then that I realized we would not have sufficient funds to make the return journey in such style and I began hoping for one of Mother's little miracles, like an acquaintance who would suddenly materialize between Calcutta and Shantinagar and lend me a couple of hundred rupees. My two accompanying friends, photographers both, were untappable. Kalyan, the keeper of our purse, had left it at home, and Teki had a hundred rupees which he had already surrendered. My mind was

far from easy as the train pulled slowly out of Howrah
Station. Mother Teresa and the young Sister sat opposite
each other by the window in prayer. I envied them.

We were out of the city, flashing through mango
orchards and palm groves and the over-burdened fields
of rural Bengal, sunlight streaming through the windows.
Inside the compartment our little party was the focus of
interest and conversation, particularly Mother in her
cheap white sari. When they ended their prayer, the
young Sister began reading the Bible and Mother a well-
thumbed copy of *Seeds of the Desert* by Charles de
Foucauld. 'It's a very beautiful book. He was a very
holy person,' Mother explained when I asked her. She
passed me the book and the paragraph I read had to
do with the need to submerge completely the ego in
the service of God. It was the moment I had been waiting for. Was it true, I asked her, that it was on a train
journey like this that God had revealed to her His wish
that she should serve Him and find Him amongst life's
derelicts?

She nodded, but I knew from experience that she was
loath to talk about herself. Yet here I was sitting next
to someone to whom God had personally spoken, and I
wanted to know about the awesome majesty of such an
experience. So I persisted. 'Mother, how did you know?
Were you not for a second in doubt? After all, Christ
Himself had moments of doubt. In Gethsemane.'

'No. There was no doubt. It was only for a moment
that He felt unsure. That was as a human being. That
was natural. The moment you accept, the moment you
surrender yourself, that's the conviction. But it may mean
death to you, eh? The conviction comes the moment
you surrender yourself. Then there is no doubt. The
moment Jesus said, "Father, I am at your disposal, Thy

will be done", He had accepted. That was His agony. He felt all the things you and I would feel as human beings. That's why He was like unto us in all things, except sin.'

But what if uncertainty remains?

'That's the time to go on your knees, eh?' And I wondered whether on that train journey to Darjeeling twenty-seven years ago this indomitable woman had sunk on her knees in prayer. For a while the powerful vision obliterated the race of fields and trees and piled clouds outside the windows. If God had spoken to us then I wonder if I would have been amazed.

'In that prayer,' she said, 'God cannot deceive you because that prayer comes from within you. That is the time you want Him most. Once you have got God within you, that's for life. There is no doubt. You can have other doubts, eh? But that particular one will never come again. No,' she said looking pensively out of the window so that I hardly caught the words, 'I have never had doubt.' And then turning to me she said with intensity, 'But I am convinced that it is He and not I. That it is His work, and not my work. I am only at His disposal. Without Him I can do nothing. But even God could do nothing for someone already full. You have to be completely empty to let Him in to do what He will. That's the most beautiful part of God, eh? Being almighty, and yet not forcing Himself on anyone.'

'But Mother, you surely have to use your initiative?'

'Of course. You have to do it as if everything depends on you – but leave the rest to God.'

'Mother, do you feel that everything is directed by God? Right and wrong?'

'There may be mistakes, many mistakes. We may make mistakes. But He cannot make mistakes. He will draw the good out of you. That's the beautiful part of God, eh? That He can stoop down and make you feel that He depends on you. The same thing with Our Lady, no? When the angel was sent to Her and said, "You are to be the Mother of Jesus," Our Lady emptied Herself and said, "Do unto me according to Thy will. I am the handmaid of the Lord." Until and unless She had surrendered, Christ would not have come into the world. There would have been no Christ, no Jesus, born. Because She was so humble, so empty, She became full of grace. At the moment She received Jesus, Her first thought was to give Him to others. She went in haste to John's house. And what did She do there? She did the servant's work. That's the most beautiful part of the goodness of God and the greatness of God's love for the world. God loved the world by giving Christ to the world, and Christ loved the world by giving His life for the world. Always giving,' she said, laughingly, 'constantly giving.'

The train rattled loudly over points as we drew into a station, upsetting its monotonous rhythm and our conversation. Raising dust.

People swarmed about the windows, urgent people searching for a seat on the already crowded train; porters staggering under heavy loads; raucous vendors selling tea in earthen pots, fly-blown sweets, cut fruits and gaudy magazines; beggars thrusting their hands into the compartments; officials gesticulating and blowing whistles. Stray dogs snarled and snapped noisily at each other. Mother read calmly through the confusion but never failed to look up and smile at the beggar children who somehow didn't seem to want more.

As we neared our destination, the lush tropical green turned to undulating scrub-land under a haze of dust

and I began to despair of ever meeting that miraculous
acquaintance who would send us happily back to Calcutta first-class. My troubles boiled over when we arrived
and Mother Teresa very practically suggested that it
would be best to buy our return tickets now. I had already discussed with Kalyan and Teki the possibility of
leaving them behind. It's amazing how something as
trivial as this should assume such exaggerated proportions in the presence of two nuns. I was sure that if
Mother knew of my predicament she would have
laughed it off and found a perfect down-to-earth solu-
tion. But, somehow, my insistence on travelling first
class had become a sinful extravagance. She had, after
all, suggested travelling second. Then, a confession here
on this seething platform would be tantamount to a lie.
Obviously the miraculous acquaintance I had hoped for
was going to be Mother T. herself. But could one ask
her for a loan? It sounded almost blasphemous. Besides,
would she have the money? And, even if she did, it
would be like borrowing from the poor-box. Happily, in
all the confusion of pushing and shoving ourselves
through the crowds and piling ourselves into a rickety
motor-van that had come to meet us, the business of
buying the return tickets was deferred.

During the half-hour drive to Shantinagar, we passed
a small scabrous concrete building that the Sister who
had come to meet us said was an abandoned leper
clinic. Mother was all attention and, in typical fashion,
was impatient to take it over. She explained that there
were thousands of lepers in the coal-mining area around
Shantinagar; the small clinic we had passed was one of
the well-intentioned but ineffectual attempts that had
been made to combat this most hideous of diseases. It
was heartening, yet strangely appalling, to hear Mother

Teresa planning yet another strategy that would send her young Sisters to work among the lepers of this desolate area.

As the green oasis of Shantinagar came into view, an extraordinary sense of anticipation seemed to possess Mother and ride with us the rest of the journey off the main highway, down a dirt road, and through a picturesque Santhali village where we paused briefly to admire the clean lines and warm earth colours of Santhali architecture. Mother expressed a desire to have Shantinagar look like that one day, and then hurriedly added, 'But you will see what wonderful work Sister Francis Xavier has done. It's a miracle, eh? She's made the desert bloom in five years.'

Sister Francis Xavier, a jovial and garrulous Yugoslav, a few years younger than Mother Teresa, welcomed us in an avenue of flamboyantly flowering trees and bustled us into a surprisingly chintzy parlour. In the Mother House of the Missionaries of Charity in Calcutta, the parlour is purely functional : a bare, polished table on which is a small statuette of the Virgin Mary, six very plain wooden chairs and some illustrated texts and charts on the wall. There is an overhead electric fan purely for the convenience of visitors. In Shantinagar, there are floral curtains and upholstered chairs, a table-cloth and flowers in a vase, and even guest towels and fresh cakes of soap in the toilet. I wondered how Sister Francis Xavier got away with it since one of the four main dictates of the Order is poverty and severe austerity. But somehow this pleasantly furnished room was in keeping with the spirit of Shantinagar which sets out to make beautiful what could be so ugly; for Shantinagar, which means 'The Place of Peace', is the fulfilment of one of Mother Teresa's most cherished dreams —

to give lepers a place of their own, a place where they can live and die with dignity, where they can work gainfully and lead lives close to normal. While there are spotlessly clean and comfortable small wards for the seriously afflicted, there are also small cottages where families can live together. For children born in Shantinagar there is a protective crèche, but wondrously there are children living with parents whose disease has been arrested and who are well on their way to recovery.

There was a young man in the shop at Shantinagar whom I mistook for a Brother, he was so cheerful and energetic.

'How old are you, John?' asked Mother Teresa. 'It's time you got married to a nice girl and settled down.'

'Twenty-one,' he said, ignoring the marriage bit.

'You're not, you're only sixteen,' said Sister Francis Xavier, 'and too young to get married yet, Mother.'

The good-hearted banter continued, with Sister Francis Xavier apparently determined not to marry John off too soon, and Mother Teresa equally determined to see him properly settled.

It came as a shock to discover that John, well-built and handsome, and with no apparent blemish on him, was a leper. We met his brother, Peter, shortly afterwards, in one of the small cottages where he lived with his wife, two children and a goat. He, too, was a leper, but, like John's, his disease had been arrested and he would soon be cured.

Sister Francis Xavier was, like Mother, once a Loreto nun. She joined the Order in 1951, bringing with her a very valuable qualification: she is a doctor. As she took us around Shantinagar, she kept introducing us to her assistants who apparently 'used the knife' with practised skill. They were all arrested lepers themselves, some looking alarmingly young to have mastered the intricacies of surgery and surgical care.

It was one of those suffocatingly hot summer days when no one in his right senses ventures out into the sun, not without a straw hat, anyway. But Sister Francis Xavier, who like Mother is an enthusiastic, well-scrubbed dynamo, led us off at a fast trot to visit the piggery, the poultry farm (where, alas, the thoroughbred hens were not doing too well), and the family cottages.

'I hope you don't get sunstroke,' she suddenly told me as we viewed the pigs. 'It's too hot for anyone to dig your grave and bury you today. It has happened before, you know,' she added laughing.

Shantinagar was made possible by a Government gift of thirty-four acres of land and generous donations from India and abroad. Mother Teresa's original plan envisaged the settling of about four hundred families, each in a small house. Apparently, she has not yet found the answer to what shape these small houses should take. She feels that the few already built look incomplete and alien to the surroundings. She said aloud that she wished they were like the lovely Santhali huts we had paused to admire.

'But Mother, those villagers have whole bodies. They have fingers and hands and feet. They can climb ladders. They can thatch and constantly renew the mud plaster. Our people cannot.'

'Yes, Sister.'

But the shape of the houses to come remains unresolved. Mother Teresa is in search of an architect who will design her inexpensive, easily-maintained huts to blend with their surroundings. She is also in search of sponsors for each family and appears confident of finding them. As she so often says, 'God will provide.'

All too soon it was time to leave Shantinagar and my problem had now grown acute. Just as we began to say our farewells, I said to Mother, 'I am in need of your help myself.' She looked startled until I explained that, having left our money behind, I needed two hundred rupees. Could I borrow it? 'But, of course,' she said and passed on the request to Sister Francis Xavier who hurried to get it.

Once again there was a group of nuns to see Mother off, and again the same deep bond between them and her became almost tangible. As we climbed into the old van one of the youngest Sisters, all schoolgirlish, began imploring, 'Mother, don't go. Mother, please don't go.' The others called out, 'God bless you, Mother', 'Come back soon, Mother', and Mother the while kept looking back through the billowing dust as we drove away. 'They are my strength,' she said simply, when I remarked on the obvious love the Sisters had for her.

It seemed our slow-moving motor-van would never make the station and I knew how much Mother wanted to get back to Calcutta in time to see off her nuns. So Kalyan was out of the van before it stopped and had bought our tickets by the time we reached the platform only to be told that our train was running four hours late. But there was another, a completely unscheduled 'workers special' about to leave for Calcutta. We just made it by scrambling into the nearest general compartment, while some Sisters who had preceded us watched despairingly from an adjoining one. We had no idea when this train would reach Calcutta but, mercifully, it took off at great speed and I couldn't help feeling that we were involved in yet another of Mother's little miracles, particularly when, at one of our few stops, we jumped off to find first-class accommodation befitting our tickets and found there was none. Retribution?

An incredulous railway official bundled us into another compartment as whistles shrilled and the train began to move. It was the compartment where the Sisters were and they were delighted to welcome Mother. It was touching to see them together. Mother, who had brought three guavas from Shantinagar, asked a Sister to share one among us, requesting that the other two be taken to the Mother House where all the Sisters might share a bit of Shantinagar. She also handed over, from her cloth bag, some slices of bread that would have been her lunch had we not eaten at Shantinagar.

At the last halt before Calcutta two cleanly dressed and beribboned children suddenly caught sight of Mother and ran up to the window clamouring with recognition. Briefly puzzled she talked to them and was delighted to discover that they had once been in her crèche for abandoned children at Howrah Station. 'They looked so different then,' she said, and I could well imagine the matted hair, the bony frames and distended stomachs characteristic of countless street orphans. The girls were now happily reunited with their parents.

Then, a very ordinary middle-aged man approached Mother and pressing some money into her hand said, 'I wish to make a present.' She blessed him as he backed away and, turning to me, said, 'That was beautiful, eh?'

We sang hymns on the way back to Calcutta, in Hindi, Malayalam, Bengali and English.

Evening was creeping into the fields about Calcutta misting distant trees and gilding such humble things as a line of bullock carts on a dusty road, oxen lazily pulling a plough and some boys bathing in a hyacinth-choked pond. Every now and then there was the distinct smell of woodsmoke which hung, shredded and still, in the groves of trees we tunnelled through. Then, suddenly, in the brown and gold and purple shadowed twilight, was a startle of vivid green field. 'It's beautiful,' said Mother Teresa. 'God's creation is beautiful, eh?'

Calcutta began to build its decaying brick about us and echoing the clatter of passing trains. As the buildings grew more dense and people thronged every lane and street and open space that flashed by, I found myself resisting a return to the city. But for Mother it was quite obviously a happy homecoming because as we hurtled past a suburban station swarming with people she began telling me of the approaching twenty-fifth anniversary of her Order. She would like to give every one of her poor a present of some kind : however small, however humble, it would help to express the love and sympathy so lacking in their lives. Then she planned to screen a film in one of the city's best cinema houses, she thought *Ben Hur*, for which the rich would buy highly-priced tickets. 'But they won't see the film, eh? They will buy my tickets for the poor. I think I can get the hall free for ten days.' This was pure Mother Teresa, thinking up the near impossible with an innocent determination to make it come about. I have known her occupy land, take over buildings and set up shop where the proverbial angels would fear to tread because she was convinced that it was necessary for 'her people' and her work. So why not *Ben Hur* for the under-privileged who never went to see a movie? On the actual day of the anniversary, 7 October 1975, Mother hoped that services would be held in Calcutta temples, churches, mosques, Sikh *Gurdwaras* and Buddhist chapels, anywhere where voices could be raised to the glory of God and for the recognition of her people.

We did arrive in time to allow Mother to see her nuns off and it would be difficult to say who was more delighted, she to see them, or they her. Next morning, impatient to return the money I had borrowed from her, we called early at the Mother House. When I produced the two hundred rupees, Mother Teresa said a puzzled thank you. She had obviously forgotten all about it and thought probably that we were making a donation.

2. Calcutta: Setting for a Mission

Calcutta, once known as the City of Palaces because of its pretentious public buildings and its extravagant private residences set in well-tended gardens, has always been a problem city. Almost from the time that it was won from teeming jungle and swamps by its unsung founder, Job Charnock, in 1690, it has attracted swarms of rural people who quickly lose whatever roots they have and become squatters either in festering slums of their own creation or in the streets of the city. Early travellers, while praising the spirit and the beauty of Calcutta, the Empire's second city, seldom failed to mention the foul and squalid city of hovels and shanties that grew fungus-like upon the City of Palaces. Kipling called it the City of Dreadful Night, 'Chance erected, chance directed'; Macaulay, 'a city where only insects and undertakers appear to enjoy the climate.' Jawaharlal Nehru saw it as a 'nightmare city'. Others have said worse because, inexorably, ever since Calcutta began, as a tentative trading-post of the East India Company, its problems have been aggravated rather than checked by the progress of civilization. It grew without plan and its purpose was money: money for the alien John Company in London, the courts of the *Nawab* in Murshidabad and the Moghul Emperor at Delhi. When the British Raj succeeded the Moghuls, Calcutta became the lucrative capital of British India: expansive, extrovert, gay, palatial, sophisticated. Always rich. Always overcrowded and, ironically, poor.

In 1947, when India became free and Bengal was divided to create East Pakistan, millions of refugees streamed into the already over-populated city. They never left. Rather, they have been joined every year and every day by other refugees from the flood, famine and drought-prone areas that form the hinterland of Calcutta. Which is why today, despite the efforts of successive State and Central Governments and massive foreign aid, Calcutta is more slum than palace. With few exceptions, the palaces themselves are now slums; extraordinary piles of decaying classical architecture in which surprisingly large numbers of people live, some gentle with gilded memories belonging to the great families that raised them, others there as tenants who have no need to keep past glories alive and so have allowed colonnades to peel, pediments to fall and standards to drop. And always, there are the squatters. So that a single grand old building can present a façade tree-sprouting and crumbling, bizarrely face-lifted and painted, or pathetically submissive to festoons of washing and the dark bruises of haphazard cooking fires.

But these are not the real slums. Because slums in Calcutta do not mean seedy tenements fallen on bad days. There are enough of those. Calcutta slums are either acres of bamboo and earth-plastered shacks with sagging tiled roofs, without sanitation and the basic amenities of water and electricity, or they are rebukes of tin and hessian and any waste that can serve as a roof. Some can hardly be called hovels, they are so mean. Then there are the open slums : the city pavements, the traffic islands, the arcades and porticoes where the homeless and the destitute find shelter of a sort. Nobody

Mother Teresa seeing off a group of nuns

When Sister Agnes was in class ten, Mother Teresa took her along on one of her visits to the Moti Jheel slum

If Calcutta is wretched, Howrah is even more so

really knows, but there are thought to be close to a million pavement dwellers in Calcutta, people who are born on the streets, live on the streets and die on the streets.

Calcutta slums are not confined to any particular part of the city so that they can be avoided or remain unseen. They are everywhere : cheek by jowl with modern city towers, prosperous shopping centres, affluent housing estates, respectable middle-class colonies, or with other slums which are a roof, a wall, or a smell better off than they.

The fact that Calcutta is vigorous, intellectual, rich and politically aware, makes its poverty all the more tragic, because this sickness of epic proportions is often taken for granted, lived with, excused, and has become an attitude of mind that wonders what better can be expected of a neglected city in a poor country. So, one can move from air-conditioned flat to air-conditioned office through festering refuse dumps and colonies of near-naked people without a twinge of conscience, without feeling and, all too often, without seeing. One can leave a restaurant, with the *maître d'hôtel* still in a tuxedo or at least a lounge suit, where the cost of a meal would keep an entire pavement family alive for months, and growl impatiently at beggars crowding outside. Or, one can emerge from Calcutta's extraordinary New Market, where almost everything and anything is available under one decaying roof, followed by porters laden with your purchases, and haggle over the scant fee they demand, let alone notice that some of them are too old or too young to work. These are not incidents out of the ordinary, and they are not intended to portray a massive callousness of spirit. In truth, they happen all the time as each well-defined stratum of Calcutta society jostles with the other. The shock, the horror, the unease, the sympathy is there but under veneers of indifference often carefully cultivated as a defence. How otherwise to live in a city piled with garbage because there are too few conservancy trucks to collect the putrefying mess, a city still menaced by open drains and hopeless lack of sanitation? Can one ever become accustomed to people bathing and defecating on the streets? A city where public hospitals are so crowded that patients lucky enough to be admitted often lie on the floor between beds and in corridors? Where the unlucky can sicken and die on city pavements?

Can one ever accept the press and whine of beggars on pavements, in markets, on railway platforms, at traffic stops, outside restaurants and cinema houses, often outside your own front door? How to accept, living in an ivory tower as I do, the unending panorama of squalor, poverty, stagnation and hopelessness just the width of a potholed road away from manicured gardens where children in frilly dresses, attended by servants, play? More to the point, how do the deprived accept us?

Then, there is the corroding climate of Calcutta fraying tempers into outbursts of mob and political fury even as it eats into steel and concrete and brick and flesh. For me, the original jungle and teeming mangrove swamps are there, just beneath the concrete and tarmacadam and behind the façade of the city. A building has only to fall and the jungle takes over. Each season brings its peculiar blight, almost old-fashioned names like typhoid, malaria, cholera, smallpox and a pestilence of diseases undiagnosed.

Foreigners coming to Calcutta are apt to suffer from culture shock in the time it takes to drive from the airport to the city centre. To them, as to at least one high-powered group of city planners, Calcutta is a dying city and the only remedy is to leave it. To most Indians, Calcutta is a strange and filthy place best avoided. Those who live in Calcutta view their city with an extraordinary love and emotion : those who have ever lived here seldom forget it, not for its filth and poverty but for its friendliness and its charm and its almost old-world graciousness, its quite incredible intellect.

To many, the transfer of the capital from Calcutta to Delhi in 1911 was a cruel shock from which their city never quite recovered. Some see it ruined by the immigration of business people from every part of India who stand accused of having exploited the locals in their hurry to prosperity. To the true Bengali, and I mean all of us who live out of choice in this grubby, cosmopolitan city, Calcutta's ills, though amply recognized and unfailingly lamented, are secondary to its charms. Of course there are the slums and the poverty and the rampant unemployment, corruption and a grievous lack of amenities. But are the monsoon clouds anywhere else so lovely and the flaming *gulmohur* and the emerald countryside more stunningly beautiful? Are people safer in the streets and in their homes anywhere else? Can any other city boast that what it thinks today culturally, politically, ideologically, the rest of India will think tomorrow? True, Calcutta has lost its industrial and business standing to Bombay and some of its political prowess to New Delhi, but it retains a capital pride all its own, a hard core of romanticism that all its poverty and dirt cannot hide.

As great cities go, Calcutta is not very old, just old enough to make its Anglo-Indian history familiarly interesting. One almost knows the grand Wellesley and the scholarly Curzon whose names are commonplace despite the fact that their statues have been removed. A tall minaret built to commemorate General Ochterlony's conquests now has another name, but the fact that every political rally of any size uses it as a forum keeps the old General alive. Warren Hastings is still remembered by a small village within the city that bears his name and one of his many residences, now a girls' college, is allegedly haunted by a ghostly carriage and an impatient Lord. King William III still lends his name to a fort in the centre of the city. One can ask a taxi-driver to be driven to Clive Street, and be promptly taken there, though long ago it was given another name. The great tank about which Calcutta first grew remains Dalhousie Square and there is a Camac Street and a Russell Street, a McLeod Street and a Ripon Street, and Kyd Street and Kidderpore named after the city's first shipbuilder. To this day, Kidderpore remains the busiest dock area. On the once fashionable Park Street, which some remember as named after Sir Elijah Impey's deer park, is the old European graveyard, an amazing garden sprouting obelisks and domes and classical pillars and pyramids all in a state of terminal decay and hardly haunted any longer by the exotic ghosts of foreign founders and master-builders of Calcutta.

Still very much alive, though often distant from the great family mansions in which their ancestors elegantly lived, are the famous families of Calcutta : the Tagores, to whom the poet Rabindranath belonged, the Ghosals, honoured by the Moghul Emperors of Delhi, the Mullicks, who still retain in fair splendour a marble palace which is an important city museum, and the Roy Chowdhrys, whose forbears leased to Job Charnock the three villages that became Calcutta. In one of these villages was the ancient temple to Kali which is believed to have given Calcutta its name and is today a renowned centre of worship. The city's largest and most famous thoroughfare, Chowringhee, keeps alive memories of Jugal Gir Chowringhee. A pious worshipper of Shiva, Kali's all-powerful consort, he was the founder of a sect known by his name.

The ravages of time, climate and history have taken heavy toll of Calcutta. Somehow an imperious but remarkably motherly Queen Victoria remains grandly enthroned outside Calcutta's most flamboyant monument, the Victoria Memorial, a monstrous confection in marble which, though a museum to the Raj, knows moments of insecurity when its future as a hospital, national library or welfare centre is mooted in overzealous sessions of State Government. Ironically, since she made no direct contribution to the city, I suspect Victoria will remain in the company of such immortals as Ramakrishna, Swami Vivekananda, Sri Aurobindo and Ram Mohan Roy. Others, who either sprang from the soil or came to Calcutta and who gave so much in their time to help the city, are more or less forgotten. Whatever became of the legion societies that set out to uplift the fallen, beautify the hideous, enrich the poor, house the homeless, feed the starving, solve the ever-growing problems of Calcutta? One can understand the almost flippant charity of a governor's lady or a group of society women fading like the season's flowers, or the message of some sudden saint being diluted by the indifference of generations, or the political promises of transient parties going unkempt.

But then, recognizing Calcutta to be the vast human quagmire it is, more surprising is the fact that anyone

or anything could leave a permanent mark upon it.
What chance, for instance, has a frail woman whose
only qualification is an unquestioning faith in God when
she sets out to bring help and love to the most wretched
of Calcutta's poor?

3. Father Henry and his Secrets

When she was twelve, Agnes Gonxha Bejaxhiu was quite sure she was going to become a nun and when, two years later, she was told of the work of the Irish Order of the Sisters of Loreto, she knew where she was going to spend the rest of her life. In India. 'It's a mission country,' she explained many, many years later, when I asked her what had brought her so far from her native Skopje, now in Yugoslavia. Born on 27 August 1910 and brought up in a large and happy Albanian family, it must have been hard to leave home and sail off to a country so unknown, so remote, when she was only seventeen. But then she had made some difficult decisions already, like deciding to dedicate her young life to God's work.

She arrived in India, like thousands of nuns before her, without fuss or fanfare and was sent immediately to Darjeeling to teach in the Loreto Convent there. At that time Darjeeling, under the British Raj, was a popular and genteel hill resort where the Governor of Bengal and all his staff and every affluent Calcuttan would repair to escape the summer heat and enjoy such Himalayan delights as promenading and riding on the Mall, dancing and dining at the Gymkhana Club or taking tea on Government House lawns and gazing unendingly at the magnificence of Mount Kanchenjunga and the romantic ranges of Sikkim and Bhutan. Darjeeling was also a premier centre of European education. So the young novice, Agnes Gonxha Bejaxhiu, who took her first vows in Darjeeling on 24 May 1931 and the name Teresa – 'The Little One' she explained when I asked which Teresa had inspired her choice – began her life in India teaching the well-to-do young.

From Darjeeling, Mother Teresa came to Calcutta, so savagely different from the hill station which reminded her in many ways of the Yugoslav countryside. The Loreto Convent to which she came stands in one of the most crowded and down-at-heel localities surrounded by slums, shamefaced factories and the marshalling yards of one of the city's most congested railway stations. Close by are the man-made mountains of the city's refuse dumps and over all, when the wind is wrong, hangs the nauseating stench of neighbouring tanneries. But Loreto School, Entally, is an oasis of well-kept buildings, emerald lawns and smartly uniformed children. The girls of Loreto Entally are, for the most part, orphans or the children of broken marriages and they come from all races and communities. Sharing the grounds of the Convent is a separate institution, St Mary's, where Bengali girls, many from the best Calcutta homes, are taught in their own language. To this school, first as a teacher and then as its Principal, came the young nun, Mary Teresa. She took her final vows in 1937 and she is remembered there still as a joyous spirit, an energetic, dynamic and totally dedicated nun.

It was to Loreto Convent, Entally, on a hot summer's day, with fans turning languidly in a comfortable parlour with its framed prints and polished wooden furniture, that we went to piece together the early days of Mother Teresa. A new and very businesslike Mother Superior, accompanied by an elderly nun, welcomed us, but added little to what we knew. 'I didn't really know her myself, and she didn't really stay here. She was in Darjeeling and at the Daughters of St Anne. They know about her there.' Her companion, turning as they left the room together, said with a sudden intensity, 'She was one of two Yugoslav nuns. Mother Gabriel, her compatriot, died in 1974. She and Mother Teresa were very close. I only know that Mother Teresa's heart was set on the work she was doing. She used to say, "I couldn't meet God if I didn't do this work." ' I thanked her and then asked her name. 'I'd rather you just mention me as one of her contemporaries.'

As we left the parlour we met a remarkably ebullient young nun who, though too young to have known Mother Teresa in Loreto Entally, was an obvious fan. We asked her if she could turn up any anecdotes, any legends. 'No,' she said, 'there are no legends. The remarkable thing about Mother Teresa was that she was ordinary.'

In the yellow-washed corridors of St Mary's, there were no memories either, but a feeling of friendly familiarity. A young Sister in a white habit surprisingly similar to the saris worn by the Missionaries of Charity sat reading outside a door that we instinctively knew led into the office once occupied by Mother.

As I have already written, over the years I have come to appreciate that Mother Teresa is loath to speak about herself. 'I am not important. Write about the work and my people,' she invariably says. When we ventured on this book and asked her if we might probe her life, her work, her mission, she said, 'Personalities are not important,' and when, on one memorable occasion we persisted with very ordinary personal questions, she said, 'That's not necessary,' and changed the topic at once. So the little we know of Mother Teresa's early life is from the surprisingly little that has been written about her and from hearsay that can be as glorifyingly exaggerated as it is often deliberately terse.

I remember how, twenty-seven years ago, when she first began her work, I was tipped off by a Catholic functionary and fellow newspaperman to 'Watch this woman, she's quite extraordinary. She's going to be a saint.' And then, only months later, after I had followed and written about her, he cautioned, 'You'd better be careful, she's seeking publicity. The Church is rather concerned.' Years later, he was to become one of Mother Teresa's most ardent champions.

By happy chance we stumbled upon a reservoir of knowledge in a church, shabby but clinging to its dignity, that by odd coincidence is dedicated to St Teresa. It stands in the same street as the Mother House of the Missionaries of Charity.

Father Henry is an old and faded man but remarkably beautiful, if 'beautiful' may be used to describe his old-world manners, his charm, his aura of godliness and even his quaint European accent. We met him on a golden evening with the sun streaming through the twin spires of St Teresa's, gilding his white hair and blurring the frayed edges of his worn white habit. He led us through a clutter of rooms where plump and dedicated ladies regularly meet together in sewing classes, where gawky young-marrieds are sat to hear the word of the Lord and where, one suspects, hopeless councils are held against encroaching poverty and dwindling faith. In an inner sanctum, stuffy from lack of use, Father Henry told us a story that at first seemed pointless to our quest.

'Every man has his limitations. And I must tell you mine. In 1913, I was on my way to Mass, joyous like all the young boys with me, when I heard the call. I would become a missionary. Go to India never to return home. Just like that. Never to return home. I come from Dampremy, in Belgium, the centre of the coal-mine area, but I'm from a family of glass-blowers. In 1938, October, I landed in India never to go home. By 1948 I was screwed down here, in charge of the Bengali community. Our church was in Entally where Mother was Head-mistress.

'We both have a secret. Only she doesn't know my secret and I don't know her secret. But it's the same secret. We are working in a parallel way. Prayer without action is no prayer at all; she believes that. So every Thursday we had a meeting to serve the country and serve the neighbour. We, that is the Sodality of Our Lady, are made up of girls from the sixth class to the eleventh class. Age twelve to twenty. From 1941 to 1947 Mother Teresa and I worked together. We have this secret. We want to work for the poorest of the poor. On Saturdays, we had social activities. We went to people in hospitals to comfort them. Or into *bustees,* the slums. Afterwards we would gather and discuss what we had learned.

'Mother has a magic in her. Her search is to experiment with God, to experience God. She got some girls from the Sodality and made them do penance and serve the country and serve the neighbour. At that time there was this beggar woman who came to Mother for help. She was given a good feed and slept in Mother Teresa's bed. Mother called her "Granny". This is loving the neighbour in action.

'Hindu and Muslim women wanted to join the Sodality and social classes. They wanted to help. That was in 1947; independence was in the air. Mahatma Gandhi had said, "Make no laws unless you consider the poorest person you know." It was an inspiration. In 1947, the Archbishop of Calcutta, Monseigneur Perier, he died at ninety, asked me, "Imagine that a European nun teaching Indian girls starts an Order to work amongst the poorest of the poor." I said, "Your Grace, that plan humanly speaking is impossible, but it is needed." He said, "If it is needed then God will bless it." At that time I left Calcutta for a retreat and I was told I wouldn't find Mother Teresa any more when I got back. You see, she still had her secret.

'Then one day a lady in a sari with a blue border comes in. "Do you recognize me?" she asks. I looked at her and said, "I seem to have seen you before." "Where is Moti Jheel?" she says, and I answer, "You should know it well; it is the slum on the other side of your Convent wall." ' He paused as the bells of St Teresa rang out and, rising, said, 'Excuse me, I will pray for a minute.' We stood with him. 'I prayed for you,' he said with a happy smile as he settled once again into the old wooden chair and, resting his arms on the dilapidated table, went on, 'Memories are the blessings of God.'

'Now, Mother de Senacle, a Mauritian nun, was Principal of Entally at that time and a great protector of Mother Teresa. She took twenty girls from Moti Jheel, the slum which is just across the wall from the Convent, and tried to educate them. After a year only two were left. It was not an atmosphere the poor were used to even though they were made at home on the verandah with a good Sister looking after them. That is why Mother Teresa had to leave the Convent.'

The story as I knew it was that Mother Teresa's room at the Convent looked out upon the acres of squalor and poverty and the unattended sickness of Moti Jheel and that she was increasingly disturbed by what she saw.

She asked permission to go into these slums with such meagre aids as she could lay hands on, a few tablets of aspirin, bandages, iodine, and the powerful will to help. Perhaps she did not know it then, but there would be no turning back. As a comparatively cloistered nun she need never have crossed the barriers between serving the poor and merging with the poor.

Father Henry's heavily accented voice cut across my thoughts. He opened one of three large, cloth-bound books with infinite care, mumbling all the while about people from his parish who had gone to war, to sea, to foreign countries to settle, who had married and had children and had died, all leaving something of themselves in these volumes, personal scrap-books of Father Henry, that were more deeply loved than parish registers.

Unbelievably, there it was, page fifty-two, illustrated with a fading photograph of a young nun in the black-and-white habit of the Loreto Order. Sadly, and yet perhaps fittingly in the context of a legend – and one shouldn't know everything about legends – time has erased the features. But she is young, you can see that, and she seems to stand hesitantly against a perfectly ordinary background of some trees and a low wall. The handwriting is large and well formed, the ink turned grey with the years is almost illegible in places : 'On the eighteenth of August 1948, Reverend Mother Teresa is leaving St Mary's, Entally, for Patna. She intends to dedicate herself in the future to the poor and abandoned people, living in the slums of Calcutta. For this very difficult work she puts all her confidence in the Immaculate Heart of Mary.' It is written in the name of 'The Society of the Missionary Sisters of Charity' and 'Agnes Concha Bejaxha'. The name as written in Father Henry's book and the name as spelled in articles one has read are at variance. I may be forgiven for not checking at the source but, in truth, I would not dare ask Mother Teresa. I can hear her saying so distinctly, 'It does not matter. It is of no importance.'

'So,' said Father Henry, 'she went to Patna, to the medical nuns, where she met Mother Denger, an American, who started the Order to heal the sick.'

Mother Teresa realized from the moment she left the sheltering Loreto convent that she needed much more than her ability to teach. There is a story that when she was still attending to the poor single-handed she was confronted by a man with a gangrenous thumb. Obviously it had to be removed. So she took a pair of scissors and, one can imagine, a prayer, and cut. Her patient fainted one way, and Mother Teresa the other. She was face to face every day with lepers, the hopelessly tubercular and sufferers from every possible disease clamouring to be cured.

'So,' said Father Henry, 'she learned a lot in Patna and returned to Calcutta, and she told Mother Denger that her Order would subsist only on what the poorest of the poor could eat. On Mondays, rice and salt, on Tuesdays, salt and rice, on Wednesdays, rice and salt, and so on. And the good Mother Denger said, "It's criminal. You will all die."

'When Mother returned she was joined by Subhasini Das, who is Sister Agnes, and Magdalene Gomes, now Sister Gertrude. They were both members of the Sodality. Sister Agnes was a small hopeless little creature. They were the short and the tall. I remember our first meal together. It was provided by God. Mother didn't want to eat, but I said, "You must." That is like her. And their programme, it was impossible. At 5.30 they were in church. By 7.30 they were already on the streets with their bags working in a sweepers' colony, visiting the sick, teaching. Mother Teresa found a small room in Moti Jheel, about nine feet by nine, and rented it for five rupees a month, where she made a school.

'One day Father Lechien, who was procurator of a mission looking after lepers, told me, "She's a mad woman." But when I met him again and asked how the mad woman was doing he said, "Make no mistake, the finger of God is there." This I already knew. She is a person of Christ, a practical experience of Christ in the poor. To her any case is a case she attends with love.'

As he spoke, Father Henry kept leafing through the books, pausing briefly over photographs and smiling at a memory. 'More and more girls were joining Mother Teresa,' he said, 'mostly girls whom she had taught in Entally, and they had found themselves temporary accommodation in the house of a Bengali Christian where,' in Father Henry's words, 'they were sleeping side by side like sardines and praying to get a permanent house.' At last Mother Teresa was offered a small, dilapidated house in the Moti Jheel slum and, according to Father Henry, 'Mother was going to make a big blunder. If she lives among all those poor demanding people, always demanding, she will disappear. Somehow it fell through, thank God.' Shortly afterwards, Mother was offered yet another old house, so old and wretched, in fact, it appeared to be on the verge of collapse. When this was pointed out to the man showing them around, he jumped up and down to demonstrate its sturdiness and promptly disappeared through the floor in a splintering of wood and clouds of dust. Apparently he died. 'And so, Mother made a novena to St Cecilia. Just then a Muslim gentleman was emigrating to Pakistan and selling his house. I went to see him and was surprised when he greeted me, "I love you." I found he knew the Jesuits well; he had studied in St Xavier's. I asked him how much he wanted and he told me to make the price myself. I offered a lakh (£7500), which was less than the price of the land, and he agreed. At that time the Archbishop was being operated upon for cataract but he recognized the urgency when I told him of the plan, and within three days the house was bought.

'When I took Mother Teresa to see the house she said, "Father, it is too big; what to do with all that?" but I said, "Mother, you will need it all. There will be a day when you will ask where to put all your people." You see, there were, in fact, three houses, not one, a beautiful place and right in the centre of town. Since then many have come there for the peace of their soul, with no religion and no theory; just to get peace.'

So this property that once belonged to a rich Muslim became, and remains, the Mother House of the Missionaries of Charity and already, proving Father Henry right, the three houses have been extended to accommodate the rapidly expanding Order. I can remember a large courtyard as one entered through the familiar black door, shaded by a vine. The vine has been replaced by the awning of a new building and the chapel is much larger but still opens on to the street so that the sounds of the city, the passing of trams and buses, cars and people, always people, for ever mingle with the prayers and sometimes drown them out, at least to human ears.

Father Henry showed us a page in his book illustrated with eleven angels and against each were written two names. One, the original name of the aspirant, the other the name she assumed when she took her vows. It was touching to find that Subhasini Das, the very first girl to join Mother Teresa, took Mother's Christian name, Agnes.

Mother Teresa and her growing family had not yet moved into the Mother House when they decided to start a home for dying destitutes. The need for one had become starkly obvious when Mother Teresa had found a woman lying on the pavement outside one of Calcutta's busiest hospitals. She was so desperately ill, that she appeared unmindful of her feet having been gnawed away by rats and cockroaches. If my memory serves, Mother carried the woman into the hospital only to be told that her precarious condition and her poverty did not allow her to be admitted. Mother Teresa's pleading was to no avail, so she set out with her patient for another hospital. One can imagine her anguish and despair when the woman died on the streets where she had been found. At much the same time, an early helper of Mother Teresa recalls how, as he and Mother once went in search of medicines for her pavement dispensary, they saw what Mother thought to be a child lying under a tree, again outside a city hospital. Returning a while later in pouring rain with the medicines, they found a pathetically wizened and emaciated man, not a child, lying dead in a mess of vomited blood. 'Cats and dogs are treated better than this,' Mother said sadly.

It had grown dark outside and Father Henry kept consulting an ancient pocket watch. No, he didn't want us to leave, he would tell us when it was time. It was just that he had to counsel some people before Benediction. He settled back into his reminiscences, hands folded, his face soft with recollection and said, 'She's the salt of the earth mixing with the earth and enriching it. But she's an obstinate woman. She has no organization. The thing about her is, "I belong to you whenever you need

me and I'll help you." She's only human. She has
human feelings. America, Australia, Africa, England,
Ceylon, wherever she goes, it is not her choice. She has
to go. She feels directed. Like a tree, her branches
spread out and give shelter.

'So now, the people of Moti Jheel gathered money to
start a small home for dying destitutes. It is called
Nirmal Hriday, the Place of the Pure Heart. They provided two beds. And one dies and one survives. That was
the rule. That is still the rule. Then people began object-
ing because they didn't like the smell of dying so they had
to close the place. Mother Teresa went to the Calcutta
Corporation and begged of them to give her a place
where people could die with dignity and love. "It is a
shame for people to die on our city roads," she told
them. The Corporation considered the question and
told Mother they had two places; one, a house not far
from the Mother House, and the other a pilgrims' rest-
house, near the great temple of Kalighat, which was
then occupied by *goondas* – thugs and loafers – who
used it as a place for gambling and drinking.

Mother Teresa chose Kalighat not, as some of her
early critics claimed, to convert people to Christianity
at the very vortex of Hinduism, but because she knew
that most of the city's destitutes go to Kalighat to die.
It is the wish of all devout Hindus in the city to be
cremated in this sacred spot.

'So we got permission,' said Father Henry, 'on the
fifteenth of August, which is India's Independence Day,
in the year 1952. "When would you like to open?" we
were asked, and Mother surprised us all by saying, "On
the Feast Day of the Immaculate Heart", which was
the twenty-second of August, just a week away. That
was the infiltration of Mother Teresa where no one else

would infiltrate. The peaceful infiltration.'

The first patient to enter the new Nirmal Hriday in Kalighat was, ironically, a woman whom Father Henry had found lying outside the same hospital to which Mother Teresa had carried the dying woman when she had just begun her work. As expected, there was opposition to Mother Teresa in Kalighat. She and her nuns were threatened. Protest from the local people reached the Corporation and the State Assembly. But, fortunately, Mother Teresa was already winning friends in higher places. There was, for instance, the 'mysterious lady', as Father Henry calls her. He saw her for the first time at the very first prize day in the small school that Mother Teresa had opened in the slums of Moti Jheel. 'Among lots of capitalistic and imperialistic ladies was a niece of the then Chief Minister of West Bengal, Dr B. C. Roy, a giant of a man and very powerful. This mysterious lady went from hut to hut in the slum finding out about Mother Teresa. What she heard made her a staunch helper of Mother till she died. She served without fuss and shunned recognition. When Mother Teresa went on retreat, it was this lady who took charge of the Home for dying destitutes in Kalighat.

'A part of Mother Teresa's soul touched her. This is something you find with Mother time and time again. It is a certain world, a realistic contact with God.'

Father Henry was consulting his watch again and there was a sound of voices in the other room, but it was obvious that the good Father wanted to tell us all there was to tell. He did so, speaking quickly and plucking memories at random. The picture he created was of a dynamic woman, an irresistible force, charged with the love of God, hurrying to do His work. A portrait spiritually powerful and yet very human.

'Dhapa is no-man's-land. It is mixture of Chinese, Hindus, Muslims, but strangely enough it is the one place in which there is no fighting in a time of communal and political troubles. People there are building houses without permission; the Missionaries of Charity had built a school in a shed for leper children. The Calcutta Corporation said, "You have to close there." What to do? Mother Teresa was in Australia. No Big Sister to ask. Somehow the people managed to get red flags and they marched to the Assembly. After an hour they came back and planted the flags about the school. The police didn't interfere.

'Nothing clever about that, just an infiltration of love. The Sisters don't bother about races and politics. Their infiltration is a simple one.

'Then in Belgachia, another big slum, there is a sewage centre and a dumping ground. There is a canal for dirty water, and the water is dirty, I tell you. And there, something happened at the corner of a dirty canal and a railway line. They built a splendid leper city. There was Mary Biswas who was in the Moti Jheel school, and when the Home for dying destitutes opened, became Superintendent there. She married a leper and said, "I will dedicate my life to the lepers." They built the colony. Leprosy is found in every class, the high and the low. The number of lepers in Calcutta is terrible.

'At Christmas they had a beautiful Mass in the leper city. They had built a church. What a Mass! Those lepers who couldn't move on their own were carried by others. It was something really grand to see.

'Then, there's Titagarh, in the industrial suburbs. Mother Teresa installed herself there. Again among the lepers. And they think she's divine because she talks to God Himself. She has complete freedom. If she didn't have it she wouldn't be able to do what she does.

'One day, there was a revolutionary meeting among the lepers and they were demanding this and that. Mother went straight there and had a meeting with the leaders, and then she came back to us, "All will be all right." On the way back to Calcutta a leper came to her and said, "Have mercy on me." He had been thrown out because Mother said all the wicked should be punished. She spared him although he was the ringleader of the revolution and all the other lepers had told him to go.

'Mother wanted leper dispensaries all over the place. So it was decided to begin with seven centres. We visited the places. One was in Moti Jheel. A councillor of the Calcutta Corporation objected, "What, so close to our house? That won't do," and he turned the Corporation against us. Mother had an idea. "We will have mobile dispensaries." And she told the councillor, "Bless you, Councillor, you have increased our efficiency ten times."

'Just then a Calcutta Corporation official, an important man, discovered he was a leper. His family chucked him out. He was not well disposed to the Sisters but they were his last resort. So he became a leper leader and helped in the administration, with Mother's blessing.

'That is Mother Teresa; to take immediate action. She has a certain instinct, a certain deep kind of wisdom. When there is a problem she takes it up and it catches fire.

'You know,' he said rising and showing us to the door, 'she's absolutely incredible. When she went to Australia she went with a broken shoulder and she once had tuberculosis. The doctors advised her not to work too hard.'

4. The First Sisters:
Poverty their Dowry

Although Father Henry knows Mother Teresa better than most, and though they both, for a while, led parallel lives doing God's work among the poor, his memories are at best selective anecdotes. They left me more eager than ever to unravel the full story of Mother Teresa, her work and her people. For instance, my earliest recollection of Mother Teresa is her attending to lepers in the slums of Howrah, a Calcutta suburb, that is in fact a twin city across the river Hooghly. If Calcutta is wretched, Howrah is even more so, more uncared for, more potholed, more sunk in its garbage, more crowded, more pestilential, a heavily industrialized area overwhelmed by pollution and unemployment. Some eighty lepers had gathered themselves in an abysmal slum cul-de-sac; the huts were visibly decayed about us, the open drains were choked with human waste and the whole place stank.

As we approached the lepers, huddled grey and limbless, we passed a boy defecating in the drain. It seemed his guts were pouring out. When I drew Mother's attention to him, she gave him a look as stoical as his own and observed that he was suffering from an advanced case of dysentery, and that she would come back to attend to him later. This, remember, was the first time I had met Mother, so I might be forgiven for mentally accusing her of indifference. It was only later that I

came to appreciate that Mother was there to attend to
lepers – their number kept increasing as the day wore
on – and that but for a single helper, a slight young
girl in a white sari, she was alone and inadequately
equipped. But she did tell her helper to get the boy's
name and address so that they could treat him later.
The extraordinary thing is that I can't remember how
we went or how we returned. I had gone to write an
article and take photographs, expecting to see yet another of those dedicated white women doing their bit
for the poor of India, women genuinely moved by the
plight of others and with the will to do something
despite their many other commitments and ties. Here I
was confronted by a foreigner not in a 'suitable' dress
or in a uniform that would somehow make her efforts
understandable, but by a woman in a humble blue-
bordered white sari. Here again I had my reservations.
Having been born and brought up in India I never
fail to feel a little uncomfortable, and very wary of
foreigners who find it necessary to wear Indian attire
to establish their sense of belonging. Besides, I've seldom
seen a European or American woman look at ease in a
sari. But there was an absolutely ordinary woman in a
perfectly ordinary sari, completely innocent of affecta-
tions who, I felt instinctively, was no passing pheno-
menon. She had the feel of permanence, of a person who
was going to continue working the way she was that day
as long as she lived. I was yet to know that she had
severed all ties; that she had dedicated herself to the
service of the poor.

So powerful, even in those earliest days of Mother
Teresa's work among Calcutta's diseased and destitute,
was her personality that one noticed little else. Try as
I may, I cannot give face or substance to the girl who

so selflessly helped Mother Teresa that day. She was very young, quiet and small. One would not have even bothered at that time to know that this nineteen-year-old Bengali girl, Subhasini Das, was Mother Teresa's first postulant, one of Mother's students from the Convent at Entally. The one Father Henry had told us about.

Sister Agnes is still small, quiet and self-effacing. She is horribly uncomfortable in the presence of interviewers, cameras and tape-recorders. Where Mother Teresa suffers these intrusions, seeing them as a necessary part of God's work, Sister Agnes shies away. She very timidly asked our photographers to stop taking photographs and requested that the tape-recorder be turned off, which is surprising seeing that she generally takes charge of the Mother House when Mother Teresa is away, as she often is nowadays. I always get the impression in the first few moments of meeting her that she feels trapped, but her hesitant smile soon warms and her practised composure gives way to friendliness. She might well have been talking about herself when she told us, 'When God wants you to do something, He gives you the strength to do it.

'I joined Mother Teresa on 19 March 1949. I was one of her students in Entally, and have known her since I was nine years old, when I first went to school. I was nearly in my last year when Mother left. When we knew she was leaving, we were all disturbed. Father Henry gave us the news saying that special permission had come from Rome and that Mother was going because God had called her to do something for the poor. We asked Father, "Why, when there are so many Loreto nuns, is our Mother called? Can't someone else go?" And Father Henry explained that nobody can be pushed into work like this. It is the call of God Himself. If one is not called by God one cannot go. We were very upset as all of us were deeply attached to her.

'She went because she had seen the suffering of the poor already from the Convent. She saw their poverty and wanted to do something to help. She asked permission from Rome to leave Loreto – it's called ex-cloistering – and she was allowed to try it out for a year. If she did not succeed she could go back to the Order. You see, she'd felt the call; she knew God wanted her to do something for the poor. She had to convince the Superior before she could write to Rome to get permission from the Holy Father to leave the Congregation. It was not easy.

'From Loreto, Mother went to Patna for four months for medical training. The Holy Family nuns are still there. They have been very good to us. They have trained many of our people. When she returned to Calcutta she was given shelter by the Little Sisters of the Poor. From there she used to go out every day carrying something : a little bread, some medicine, things like that. And she used to walk from slum to slum to slum. Always working. And always she would go to St Teresa's to pray and eat the little food she had left, if any; she probably gave it all away.'

Like Mother Teresa, Sister Agnes was reluctant to talk about herself, even to confirm that she was the first to join. She dismisses their early difficulties by stressing that God gives one strength in the knowledge that 'whatever you are doing for the poor you are doing for Christ.'

'It was like that for Mother, leaving Loreto where she was leading a comfortable life for the uncertainty of the streets. She didn't know where she was going, or what she was going to do in the future. Nothing. But she was not frightened. She knew God was calling her and would lead her where He wanted. One thing very outstanding is Mother's faith. She came blindly, trusting in God, not knowing where she was going to live or from where food would come.

'Always, when I am worrying about tomorrow, Mother scolds me and asks, "Why? Isn't God looking after us?" And this we have to learn from Mother. She says that anything we have or want to keep we should give away while we have it. But we are always worrying about what will happen when things finish, but has God ever failed us? Hasn't He seen that we get what we want in time? Amazingly, it's true. Because during the twenty-six years we've had our Congregation we've fed so many people daily without having an income of our own. Everything runs on the charity of the people. God touches their hearts and they come and give.

'Nowadays we are being helped by a lot of organizations, but in the beginning we had none of these. When we started Mother used to bring a tin and announce in the parish, "Don't throw away your food." The Sisters used to go out with similar tins and collect left-overs and give them to the poor people. We used to go from house to house. Now we have CARITAS and the Food-for-Work programme, but we do not always observe the rules. How can we? There are so many people. Can we tell them not to come? Sometimes we are giving food to people who cannot work. How can you turn away someone who has not eaten for a day? You have to give something. It is very pathetic. You can die of disease, but to die bit by bit, starving, there cannot be anything worse than that. At the Sealdah and Howrah Stations people come from villages where there is no hope of getting any food. You see them day after day lying in corners just waiting for death. Mother is so humble. Even when she goes on planes she asks for whatever food is left over – "Whatever food you can give me please give me, I will carry it." '

We could not meet Sister Gertrude who followed Sister Agnes into the Missionaries of Charity just a month later. She is presently in the Yemen in charge of the Missionaries of Charity home there, but we did meet Sister Florence who was among the first girls to join. Like Sister Agnes, she had been a pupil of Mother Teresa's at Entally and came from a Bengali family. When she was in class ten, Mother Teresa, who was still Principal of the school, took her along on one of her visits to the Moti Jheel slum over the Convent wall. There, as they walked amidst the filth and poverty that must have appeared oppressive to a young girl from a well-to-do background, Mother Teresa explained to her young companion how necessary it was that someone should care for these under-privileged people. They must have been inspiring words, words not so much calculated to impress profoundly a sensitive young girl, but words coming straight from the heart of a woman deeply moved and already aware of God's need for her. Would young Agnes Vincent, now Sister Florence, come and give a helping hand if someone began such a service? And the young girl answered, 'Yes, Mother. Surely we will be able to help.'

'But supposing your parents object?'

'No, Mother, I am sure that by God's grace my parents will not mind.'

Agnes Vincent was not the only girl Mother Teresa was inspiring. There were others, all senior girls, whom she used to take with her one at a time into the slums, and to each of them she put the same question : would they help a service dedicated to the poorest of the poor? Would their parents object?

'She was testing our minds,' said Sister Florence, 'inspiring us, giving us encouragement. Always from the terrace of our school she could see the slums. I suppose we knew she'd be leaving. When the time came, we gave her a farewell. We sang something beautiful in Bengali – they were farewell songs. The children gave her something and everybody was in tears. From the reception I think she went to the church and from there she left. We didn't see her any more. We heard she'd gone to Patna for medical training, and then that she was back and had started working amongst the poor. Soon she came fishing to our homes, talking to our parents and to us. We were sitting for our School Final exams then, so our parents thought study was more important than anything else. But Mother said, "No, no, the sooner you come, the better." She was young-looking and very dynamic. She inspired us. So we joined her, Sister Agnes first, then Sister Gertrude and Sister Dorothy. We went two and three at a time and formed a group. There were twelve of us without Mother, exactly like the Apostles. Then one left because she found it was not her vocation. Four of us carried on studying for our School Finals after joining Mother and she used to coach us to make sure we passed.

'There was one other person with us, an old Bengali lady who used to work in the Entally Convent. She had been there a long time as a cook. She was very fond of Mother, so that when Mother decided to leave, she left too. Mother needed someone to help her. We all know her as Charu's Mother, which is the custom in Indian families. You know how it is, a married woman is first called the wife of so-and-so, later the mother of so-and-so, never by her own name. She's old and retired now but one of her grandsons is coming to make his postulation with the Brothers.'

Sister Florence, with the reticence of all Mother Teresa's nuns, didn't exactly say so, but we gathered that those early days were difficult ones and relieved from crippling uncertainty only by Mother's faith. 'Mother always said God will provide. Even in the beginning when visiting friends and relatives used to bring us something she would say, "No, there is no need. God will provide." But sometimes, just to make our parents happy, Mother would agree to them bringing uncooked food as otherwise it might taste too delicious. Once I remember my mother wanted to bring us some *hilsa* fish cooked in the traditional way. That's a great Bengali delicacy, you know. Mother Teresa at first said "No." But then, when she saw my mother was upset, allowed it to be boiled, just boiled. Even now, on feast days only are our families allowed to bring us something to share with the other Sisters. It is wonderful that God always provides what is necessary for us. Sometimes He gives us more than the poor people we are looking after. Which shows, really, that He is looking after us for looking after His poor.'

Sometimes it seems God offers the Missionaries of Charity so much they see fit to refuse Him. 'When it is against our spirit,' Sister Florence explained. 'For example, somebody wanted to give us a washing-machine. Mother called us all together because she wanted to see our minds. All of us refused. We said, "No, we prefer to wash our own clothes." So, until now, we do not have a washing-machine. That's like the telephone. In the beginning Mother wouldn't have one. When she saw how important, how necessary it was for our work and our people, she allowed one in the Mother House. And we do not have fans except in the parlour and sometimes in the chapel for outsiders who come to pray there. There's plenty of God's good breeze. When the people of the world are suffering so much ours is nothing by comparison.'

'Sister Florence, have you ever looked back or ever thought that you might have enjoyed doing something else?'

'I have never doubted,' she said without hesitation. 'In this calling there always are some trials. But Mother is always there to help us with her kindness and her spirit of love . . .'

'These are rapidly changing times, Sister. You, being among the first to join Mother Teresa, have helped in twenty-five years of her work. What do you think of the future of your Order? Do you believe it will be carried forward with the same faith and zeal?'

'Yes, I have no doubt, and that is why every now and then we have renewal. We see if there is a worldly spirit creeping in that is against our poverty; we try to correct ourselves, we must correct ourselves. In the beginning we had strict poverty, absolute poverty, like the poorest people. But the Holy Father, I think, did not want such poverty. Mother realized that we had to be healthy enough to do our work properly. In matters like this Mother has the last word, but she always consults us.'

Sister Bernard, one of the original twelve, accompanied us to the leper hospital and rehabilitation centre at Titagarh in the industrial suburbs of Calcutta. Titagarh is jute and paper and power, with its face to the river Hooghly and its back to beautiful Bengal countryside

where the slums leave off. We motored, it seemed end-
lessly, through a threat of decrepit buildings, some grand
and florid in the old Colonial style, some plainly hideous,
a late-Victorian architect's idea of what European
suburbs in industrial India should look like, and the rest
a shambles of wretchedness. Yet somehow this enormous
sense of decay is both relieved and emphasized by a ballet
of people, stray cows, dogs and vivid bursts of fruit and
flower vendors, sweetmeat stalls and pedlars selling
geegaws. It's amazing how, against the natural lavish-
ness of Calcutta – trees growing from mossy crannies
in the city, or green trees against lush fields against
hyacinth-covered green ponds in the countryside – a
single pedlar with his tatty wares can assume a 'com-
manding magic. He's a Pied Piper for the children. A
stab of nostalgia for the old.

Sister Bernard and a companion sat quietly in the
front seat of the car throughout a long ride but, as we
turned off the main road, down a lane between a claustrophobic row of shanties built on stilts above open
drains, they responded to calls and waves of recognition.
We knew we had arrived at yet another oasis of the
Missionaries of Charity. As we stopped in front of a
rambling temporary structure of brick, tin and bamboo, a
train shrieked across an embankment behind it. Sister
Bernard, in the simple act of stepping out from the car,
stepped into her own. We followed her and were immediately swallowed by deep shade. My companion,
Dubby, had a professed horror of disease and death
and it had been something more than ordinary persuasion
that had brought him to Titagarh with us. But if we
both had qualms about being pushed willy-nilly into a
horrifying situation, we were comforted by a quite
extraordinary feeling of the familiar. There, lying in

rows, were sick and some horribly disfigured people being attended to with everyday casualness. Most of those who helped were lepers themselves, carrying medicines, mugs of water, or even performing miracles of minor surgery. Almost certainly it was the radiant confidence of Sister Bernard that made the transition from the robust world outside to this so easy.

She was already talking cheerfully to the patients and introducing us to them. 'This is Sajada,' she said, gesturing towards a tall, very dark man whose face had been gnarled by disease and who met our greetings with measured, cold eyes. 'He's a murderer,' said Sister Bernard cheerily, 'he has been in prison. He's deformed but he has a heart of gold. When he gets into a temper there is nothing under the sun he's not capable of. Yesterday, he was in such pain that he took a blade and cut all around one of his sores. He performed his own little operation, then came to us. He's been here a long time. About ten or twelve years. You see, he keeps coming and going. He does all kinds of illegal things like brewing liquor and making bombs. People hire him and pay him very high rates. Only yesterday he told me, "You Brothers and Sisters have defeated me. You love even the wicked, but I am paid to finish them off." He is quite lovable really. He talks very eloquently and speaks the truth. He admits to drinking heavily and boasts that he will get even with the fat, rich parasites of society. Sometimes he stays with us only a few days while he has the pain. Then he runs away.'

As we walked with Sister Bernard among her patients, she chattered about how the Missionaries of Charity had begun their work in Titagarh. As in so many industrial areas, there is a lot of leprosy around and much of it goes untreated because there is nowhere to go and so

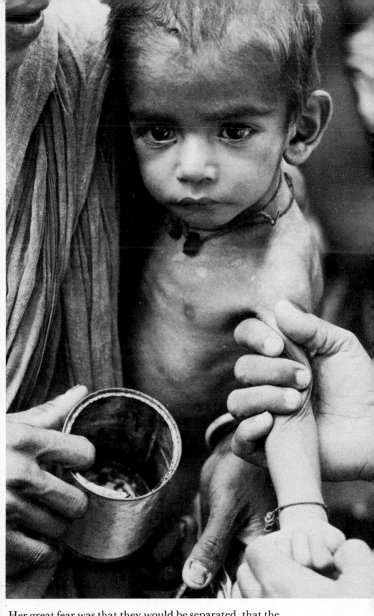

Her great fear was that they would be separated, that the child would die

The children come at you inviting affection, tugging at your clothes. 'The babies must not die uncared for and unloved.'

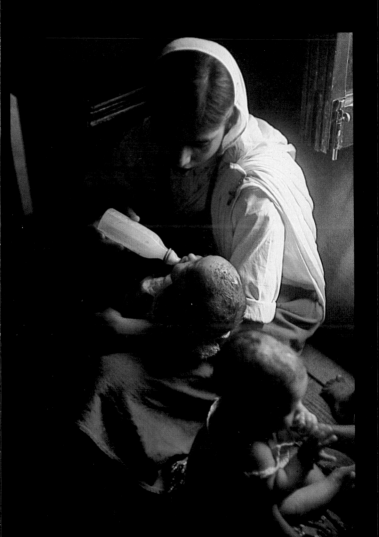

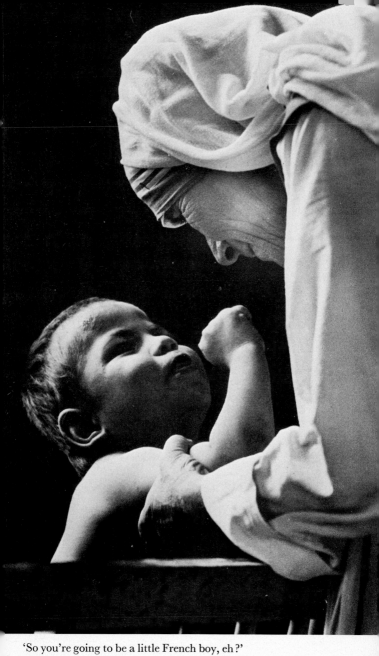

'So you're going to be a little French boy, eh?'

much fear attaches to the disease. Even when people are ready to help it is difficult to find a place to set up centres. 'Because,' said Sister Bernard, 'nobody wants lepers around. They are all terrified. This is unoccupied land belonging to the Railways. In the beginning, about twenty years ago, we just occupied it and have started extending along the railway line and we are hoping to create a colony where leper families can build their own homes and tend their own fields. But it is dangerous because our more maimed people are sometimes unable to avoid the passing trains. We have had some accidents. The Railways have generously given us land elsewhere but this remains unoccupied and since they are not making use of it we are extending.' Dramatizing Sister Bernard's words was a constant rush of trains which caused the flimsy structure to shudder.

Apart from the Centre itself, there were tiered, bamboo-walled structures running parallel to the railway line, within a few feet of it, where lepers were being taught to weave cloth and bandages for themselves and make paper bags for their own medicines. All of it looked tragically vulnerable to the weather and Sister Bernard confirmed that during the monsoons the rain came right in, but since they are squatters they cannot build more permanent structures.

Thousands of lepers have been treated in Titagarh since the Centre began. Only those with advanced ulcers and those who are highly positive and infectious are admitted as indoor patients. Others come for treatment. There are about five thousand at a time attending the outdoor clinic and, on an average, one thousand new cases are registered every year. The response to the modern treatment the Centre provides is encouraging. Many patients are completely cured. But, according to

Sister Bernard, lack of education prevents many from being healed.

'They don't continue the treatment we give them. They leave long gaps during which time the disease worsens. You see, it's a long treatment and always there is the sad fact that poor lepers have nowhere to live. Their own people don't accept them. Oh yes, there are rich lepers. We have people like students from university and from very well-to-do homes and well-known families who come to take medicine. We had a girl about to get married who came here quietly to be cured. Her family had found that she had a leprous patch and they knew that if her in-laws-to-be discovered it they would never allow the marriage. Fortunately, she was cured.

'Then recently we had a little boy, about twelve, who told us that one day, while studying, he found his fingers getting stiff and crooked. There was no patch on him but he was a leper all the same. It's a nerve disease and once the nerves are affected they cripple and it is difficult to do anything at that stage. The disease can be arrested; restoring the nerves is almost impossible. That's how the terrible scars and ulceration come about. Lepers can't feel heat or pain in their extremities so they are often badly burned and maimed. Then the decay sets in. Age is no barrier; anyone can have it. We have found many little children who are highly positive cases. We have had a six-month-old baby with a leprous patch.

'When you come to know leprosy patients, they are so nice. So great. And we learn much from them. You know what they say sometimes? "We have leprosy outside, physically, but not on our hearts." And they're very affectionate because we come into such close contact with them.'

We noticed a young man, obviously a foreigner, working quietly in a small dispensary. He was very pale, wan almost, and his white doctor's coat hung loosely about him. 'He's from Ireland,' said Sister Bernard. 'He was in Africa for eight years before coming to India to work among leprosy patients. He has asked for permission to stay and we hope he can. What is so wonderful in his life is that he has understood universal love : at his age. He is not very old. He speaks of this universal love, the love that goes out to all. He came and told me once about a mother who had thrown her son out of the house because he had leprosy. If she had known that universal love she would have accepted her son in spite of the disease.'

It was universal love that brought Sister Bernard, then the student Beatrice D. Rozario, from Loreto Convent in Entally to join Mother Teresa. On her own admission, her family did not like the idea. 'You see, at least now Mother's a name. You read about her in the papers. At that time she was nothing at all. We just joined blindly. Nowadays you see girls on the road, going to school and college and moving about on their own. At that time girls didn't have so much freedom and they hardly used to go to slums to work with the poor.'

'Sister Bernard, did your family give you up?'

'They had to. Anyone who becomes a nun or a priest has to be given up. But we weren't ordinary nuns. Ours was a different kind of work altogether, among people neither valued nor respected in society. That we should spend our time and our lives working for the poorest, working with lepers . . . how could they understand? At that time we ourselves didn't understand the seriousness of it. There was no shape and size to the work. We never thought that there would be a Home like this or a school like that. As the requirements came we just started doing the work.

'We realized that there were a lot of undernourished children and poor dying people that the hospitals could do nothing for. How many can they take? And besides, medicine alone is not enough. We just used to try and bring them a little relief on the streets. When they died we used to inform the police. For five years we did that, then Mother realized we had to open a home.

'We were always begging for medicines. Mother used to beg from various Missions, from her friends, from anybody. Now at least she receives donations, at that time she was unknown. She was almost on the street herself.

'We had to manage with the bare minimum. And Mother really had to train us, the first group, so that the others would be able to follow. Now, when we tell these other Sisters how we, in the first group, lived, they can't believe. They say it's incredible. It was. It must have been.

'We had to wash our clothes every day because we were in contact with infectious diseases. We used the cheapest soap in the market. We used to think that washing-powder was for the rich. Remember, most of us were studying in College at the time. Our Order had not yet been started. Rome only gave permission in October 1950.

'We were wearing the plainest white saris, like our novices do now. Mother was about thirty-five, thirty-six. She was very energetic. Now she is old and cannot manage that much, but she is still very dynamic. She used to teach and train us at home and manage the work outside. She never showed us she needed extra help outside. She just told us, "You are students. Go and study." We gave her a helping hand of course, but she never felt helpless on her own. It was tough. And she wanted it to be tough. She didn't want to make it easy and she was not arbitrary with her ideals, her charismatic gift. She was moving around and doing things, so she didn't notice the hardship. She had no intention of noticing. She knew it was part of our training. Even now, in Mother House, where we are nearly two hundred and fifty to three hundred strong, she could make things easy for us in so many ways. But she doesn't. It is meant to be, it has got to be a hard training. Sisters can be sent anywhere. The hardship and difficulty is never calculated, otherwise there wouldn't have been all this. It would not have been possible.'

'Sister Bernard, I seem to remember you had little to eat in those early days.'

'No, that's not true. We had the cheapest food, poor food, but Mother made us eat plenty so we didn't have to depend on other expensive nourishing things. Mother was always afraid that we might get TB or things like that. But we kept good health.

'Our first constitution was that no one could stay at home, not even to cook. So we used to take turns to cook a little in the morning and the rest when we came home. Now some stay at home for office work and to receive phone calls and guests and visitors. That is because the work has expanded so much.'

'Sister Bernard, how do you spend your day?'

'We wake at four, pray till half past six, and then have our first meal. We do our own washing and cleaning of the House before we go out to work. The novices come home for lunch and prayer. They rest a little then have regular classes, studying the rules and scriptures. They have tests before they are professed. We come home at half past twelve, go out again at two, then come in again by half past seven. We have to be back for prayers – this is very important. Mother doesn't want the Missionaries of Charity to see themselves simply as social workers. By no means.'

'Sister Bernard, where did you stay when you joined Mother Teresa?'

'We were in a house in Creek Lane. A very narrow lane close to Nilratan Sarkar Hospital. We were given the second floor, about four or five rooms. It was so central we could go to the slums easily from there. It was the home of Mr Michael Gomes.'

5. Michael Gomes: In the Beginning

We went to find Creek Lane, which meanders through tired, often quite magnificent, old buildings, like the creek from which it took its name once did. Though right in the hurly-burly of Calcutta, Creek Lane has an old-world quiet all its own and a down-at-heel graciousness of fine gateways set in high walls over which bougainvillaea and other creepers pour; of pillared porticoes and well-proportioned houses with shuttered windows under classical pediments. The old gas standards have been electrified, but the past, particularly in the evenings, lies around in pools of deep shadow. So a passing rickshaw may be mistaken briefly for a palanquin, and a parked car for a carriage.

We went to look for Michael Gomes in the evening. In a teeming city Creek Lane was empty enough for us not to find people to enquire after the house. By a strange coincidence, the first person we saw was a nun in the familiar blue-bordered white sari being pulled through the shadows in a rickshaw. But no, she wasn't a Missionary of Charity and she didn't know where the Gomes family lived. A little boy who suddenly materialized took us to the place, down yet another even narrower lane, past a pretentious mansion with plaster lions prowling on its high gates and a temple to Shiva thrusting its spire above a darkness of tall trees, to one of those buildings so elegantly typical of the once well-to-do Calcutta gentry with its tiered arches, its extravagant plaster ledges and its watchman's alcove at the gate. I felt we were at the wrong place. It looked too impressive. So we climbed the stairs hesitantly after the impetuous boy until we came upon the pictures : a Virgin Mary, Christ of the Sacred Heart and then an amateurish water-colour of Mother herself. The boy disappeared through a large doorway and we were left standing rather embarrassed in a spotlessly-kept verandah.

It might help to explain here that none of us pursuing the story of Mother Teresa is Catholic. Raghu Rai is a Punjabi Hindu, but not overly religious; similarly, my friend Dubby. Kalyan is a Hindu from the Kumaon Hills and young enough to be fiercely traditional when he remembers. I was baptized in the Protestant Church of St James's within a stone's throw of where we stood. But I have lived long enough with the great religions of India for much of them to have rubbed off on whatever original faith I had.

Lights were switched on in the room into which the boy had disappeared and a shy, slim, bespectacled man in his fifties invited us inside. Mother Teresa has described Michael Gomes as a very holy man, and it shows in his gentleness and his serenity. We had made no appointment, it could have been the most inconvenient time to call, and it stood out a mile that with our cameras and tape-recorders we were not on a social visit. He asked us to sit down and ordered tea. When we told him what we wanted, he seemed to consider for a while and then, almost reluctantly at first, began to answer our questions.

Yes, the house was old, it was ancestral property. Four brothers shared it but, in 1947, when Bengal was partitioned at the time of Independence, two of them had gone to the newly-formed East Pakistan. They had gone

on the advice of the Archbishop of Calcutta who felt
they would give heart to the Christians there. The eldest
brother knew Mother Teresa because his daughter was
studying at Loreto Entally and Mother was teaching
her. But Michael Gomes didn't know her then; his
introduction came later in one of those strange ways
in which the hand of God is often seen.

His mother was seriously ill and Father Henry came
to give her the Last Sacraments. While he was there he
asked if Michael Gomes knew of a place, a small room,
a hut, anything would do, where Mother Teresa, then
in Patna, could begin her work among Calcutta's poor.
She had expressed a desire to live in a poor locality. The
rest of the story is best told by Michael Gomes.

'My daughter, she was very small then, heard Father
make his request and said, "The whole upstairs is empty.
Do you want to see it?" And Father said, "Yes." But
after he had looked around he thought it was much too
big. All he wanted was a room. This whole floor where
we now sit was empty because my brothers were away,
but there were furniture and belongings stacked about.
So Mother Teresa came and occupied this room where
we are. She brought empty deal-wood boxes and a
packing-case as her desk. She brought a suitcase and a
chair. That's all she had. When she needed something
she called us and we told her she was free to use what
furniture she liked.' What Michael Gomes did not tell
us, but Mother Teresa did, was that he refused to accept
either rent or money for food and the numerous other
things he provided in those early, bleak days. He took
nothing. But he and his family, like those who opened
their homes and hearts to a stranger and his disciples
almost two millennia ago, will be remembered as having
helped to kindle a sacred flame that is already sweeping

the world. Only, his humility would not allow Michael Gomes to see it that way.

'All the time the Congregation was growing. One day, Mother sent me a note saying that one of the Sisters was coming in for chicken-pox and it was necessary to segregate her and could she have another room. Then it was something else, and something else, until slowly she used the whole floor. There was a difficulty about bathing as there were only two bathrooms and there were now about thirty of them. Then one day some builders from St Teresa's parish came with bricks and bamboo matting and put up some bathing cubicles on the roof. The girls used to enjoy themselves because you could hear their laughter all over the house and from the top of the road.

'Now the enjoyment is a bit less, I think. They have a huge House and a lot of people. Here, they used to run and play hopscotch and tug-of-war, but they had a discipline, a bell system. When the bell rings, they have to go out; a bell rings and they eat and pray. Those were hard days. They worked a lot and they had to study a lot because once they joined, they joined, there was no going home, which is the procedure still followed. Mother used to coach them if they were attending school or college. I remember Sister Gertrude, who is now in the Yemen, had matriculated before joining. Mother wanted her to go for the Bachelor of Medicine course. They needed a doctor badly, but she didn't have the requisite Maths. So Mother had her given a crash course and she was admitted to the Intermediate Science course.

'There was a time when she had no food for herself. They used to go begging from door to door and there were people who just turned their backs. But God helped them. It came. It came. Something always turned up. There was the time when she started her first school and a person came to give her some money and Mother asked what it was for and he said, "For a school." I brought out the receipt book but he didn't want a receipt. "I will come back later for one," he said, but he never came back.

'Our first school was started in Moti Jheel, that's the big slum near Loreto. It was just an open space among the huts. No blackboards, no benches, no chairs, nothing. Just an open space. Mother got one of the labourers, who was doing nothing, to knock the grass off with a spade and, taking a stick, began writing on the ground, in the mud. She wrote the Bengali alphabet, said a prayer, and started with some nursery rhymes. The very second day someone donated a table, then a chair, later a cupboard.

'From the beginning she started attending to dying destitutes right there on the streets where she found them. There was nowhere to take them. She asked me if I knew anyone who would give her medicines. The Fathers at St Teresa's were good enough to give her a corner for an outdoor dispensary. Crowds of people came. Now, I knew someone who might give her medicines, but we had never met. "We have spoken only on the phone," I told Mother.

'Mother said, "That's good enough," so we went, and he jumped on his chair when he heard that we wanted things free. He made a list and said he would try and get everything at a big discount and told us to come back in two days' time. When we returned, he gave us five parcels of medicines, all that we had asked for and more. And he told her to pay nothing.

'We saw a man die on the streets that day in the rain

all alone. Mother was very moved and was all the more determined to start a home for dying destitutes. Within two months she managed to get a place back to back with the famous Kali temple. It was a rest-house for pilgrims, particularly those who came from outside Calcutta. A rich merchant used to provide for their food and even their clothes. But it had become a den of gamblers and drug addicts and of ill-fame.

'For a few months after taking it over, Mother had a bad time. There was brickbatting and threats and a continuous shower of stones.

'The young men of the locality went to the local Congress Committee and complained that a foreign lady was converting the poor to Christianity. They all went to the Police Commissioner and demanded that she be pushed out. The Commissioner gave his word but he said he must first see things for himself. When he went, Mother was attending to a patient who had cancer or something and she was putting potassium permanganate on his sores from which maggots were coming out. The stench was terrible. How the Sisters bear it only God knows. Now Mother, in spite of her preoccupation, felt that the man had come for some purpose. If he wanted to look around, she would take him. He said no, he would see things for himself. And he did. In the meantime a group of boys had come in and were standing around Mother as she worked. When the Police Commissioner saw them he said, "I have given my word that I would push this lady out and I will keep it. But, before I do, you must get your mothers and your sisters to do the work she is doing. Only then will I exercise my authority." They were all stunned. Then he added, "At the back of this place is a black stone image of the goddess, Kali. Here is the living Kali."

'Now, though the Police Commissioner did his utmost to give Mother protection, the threats and the stones kept on coming.

'One day, Mother saw a crowd on the pavement outside the Kali temple and in their midst was a man dying in a pool of mess. No one would touch him as he had cholera. Mother herself picked him up and took him to the Home where she nursed him and cared for him. Eventually he died, but he had a happy death. He was a priest in the Kali temple. And after that there was no more trouble. There have been many cases like that.

'There was a man working in the docks, an ordinary tally clerk, and he was watching goods being unloaded when the chain snapped and a huge bale fell on him. He didn't die. An ambulance was sent for and he was rushed to hospital. There a doctor told the ambulance stretcher-bearers to lift the stretcher on to the bed. They objected, saying that it was their stretcher and they must remove it. When the doctor explained that the man could not be moved any more, that he had had enough, the stretcher-bearers began arguing and refused to heed the doctor. And that man literally started walking. He just got up and started walking away. He was almost dead but he was shouting and howling and abusing the whole time. They couldn't control him so they went and brought his father to quieten him. It didn't work.

'Now, from the beginning, Mother used to send her Sisters to visit the hospitals. So two Sisters were standing near the man and saw the incident. When he saw them he began taunting them in Bengali. They understood but went to help him and got him to lie down.

'When they came to visit him next, gangrene had set in. As he saw the Sisters he began shouting, "The nurses don't come near me. They catch their noses and cover their mouths and run away. No one comes near me. No one. Why are you tending to me without catching your noses? Don't you get the smell?" The Sisters said, "Yes, we get the smell, but we are thinking about your suffering. What you are going through must be excruciating agony. Compared to that, the smell is nothing. It doesn't count.'

'The man was touched by their sympathy and asked if he could go to their hospital. When the Sisters said they had none, only a place for dying destitutes, he said he would like to go there. He would be happy to die there. So they took him to Kalighat and his father went with him. Next morning, Mother Teresa found the old man crying. She asked what had happened, had someone ill-treated him? He said no, it was just that his son who had been howling and abusing for the last few days was suddenly quiet. "I think the end has come, that's why I am crying." '

A pretty, plump woman dressed in a sari brought in tea and platefuls of sandwiches. Michael Gomes introduced her as his daughter and the children who followed as his grandchildren. For a moment, as she left the room, passing beneath a large illuminated statue of the Sacred Heart in a glass cabinet, I was reminded powerfully of another woman who had bustled through this room and I could almost hear laughter coming from upstairs. There was the sudden thrill of being where something so wonderful had begun; in this very room with its many doors, its old-fashioned furniture and its memories. One must have been particularly painful for Michael Gomes : a photograph of his niece as a Missionary of Charity. She had died young.

'Mother was only thirty-five when she started,' Michael Gomes said, when tea had been cleared. 'It seems strange because since 1948 she never seems to change. She always looks the same, a little older, sometimes worried . . .

'Her first real work was teaching. That's why she started with a school. According to her Congregation rules, they don't go out alone, always in pairs. When she had no Sisters, she used to take my daughter and my niece. She would go out at eight in the morning and return for lunch between twelve and one. One day she was very late and, naturally, my wife was alarmed. When they came back, Mother was drenched through, but the first thing she said to my wife was, "Sorry, the girls are wet." When my wife pointed out that Mother was even more wet, she remarked that it was nothing compared to what they had seen that morning in a slum they had visited. In a demolished hovel they had found a woman with a child on her shoulder. And the child had a raging fever. The woman was standing in water that reached higher than her knees and she was holding a broken enamel bowl over the child's head. And all because two months' rent had not been paid, just eight rupees (40 pence), for that miserable room. Despite the rain, the landlord had sent his men to tear down the roof and drive the woman out. "That child had one-hundred-and-four degrees fever," Mother said, "I must go back at once and see what we can do. Imagine, just for eight rupees that child is dying in the rain, and whatever few things they have are floating in the water."

'On another occasion, the Sisters brought me a child. He had a stomach-ache, they said, because he had eaten some rubbish. So I sat the child down and asked him what he had eaten. In the morning? Nothing. Last night? Nothing. All yesterday? Nothing. The pain was due to hunger.

'You know,' he said, pausing as if to choose his words with special care, 'I think the only thing that keeps Mother going is her strict self-discipline and, of course, her great belief. She has tremendous faith. She keeps on yearning and working with an objective. When she doesn't get it, she's quite happy. She says, "It doesn't matter, it is God's will." That's her way . . . She's been criticized, you know. She's accused of not answering letters, not immediately acknowledging donations. They say she has no business sense. I say she is alone. She has to do everything herself. She has to work all day and sit up at night writing. How can she do it?

'One day she tells me, "Michael, the Government is giving me thirty-three rupees per child in my Home for children and I have accepted it." I was surprised. I said, "Mother, I wonder if you will be happy with a Government grant because I have worked with the Government and know what it means. According to the rules and regulations you will have to have a committee to meet twice a month. You will have to maintain complicated accounts on all sorts of things." Now she was surprised and said, "Why don't you like it? We'll have a small committee of friends, like the Police Commissioner, that's all." That's typical of Mother.

'After about six months I met her on the road one day and she said, "You know, Michael, I've been singing all the way back from the Government headquarters." "Where were you singing, Mother?" "In the tram-car. I told them today I didn't want their grant. You were right. It will be too much trouble. Besides, they insist that I spend thirty-three rupees on every child. But I spend only seventeen rupees on our children and there are so many of them. How can I spend thirty-three rupees on some and seventeen rupees on others? Who can work a thing like that?" That's Mother.

'You know, there was an evening like this when we were sitting and waiting for Mother to come back. She had gone to collect a consignment of food. Suddenly, there she was, coming down the lane, riding on top of a lorry piled with bags of flour. She was just sitting there meditating and saying her prayers. When I asked her why she bothered to go herself on jobs like this, she said that if she didn't most of the things would get stolen. If she sent the Sisters, they would have to go several times. But with her the authorities are very good. She has a point. So many things get stolen in transit. She told me that once, when she got nine ambulances from Britain and went with the British Deputy High Commissioner to receive them, they found the tool-kits from five of the ambulances missing. Mark you, she goes out at eight in the morning and returns at four or five o'clock in the evening without even a drop of water.

'Sometimes she has to be forced to go to bed. About three years ago, she was actually forced into a nursing home. She was close to a breakdown and the Sisters were greatly alarmed. She was physically very tired and was kept going only by her tremendous faith. She broke a leg once, in Darjeeling, and Mrs Gandhi, the Prime Minister, went to visit her. She's a good friend of Mother and the Missionaries of Charity. In Delhi, the Prime Minister used to phone up their House there and tell the Superior that she had a lot of vegetables in her own garden or sent in as gifts. Would they be useful? She would then have them sent over. There's the other side. One day, a Government Minister sent the Delhi Superior a note asking her to give four foreign-donated blankets to his driver. She took the note and just wrote across it, "These blankets are meant for the poor."

'Which reminds me of the refugee camp outside Calcutta when millions of homeless people were pouring in from Bangladesh in 1971. Senator Edward Kennedy paid a visit to Calcutta and the Government had drawn up a programme for him. But he wanted to see things as they were so he asked to visit the camp. Officials and people milled around him wherever he went, so it was difficult for him to see much. But suddenly he spied something : a Sister was washing clothes from the cholera ward. It was Sister Agnes, and Senator Kennedy asked if he might shake her hand. She said that her hands were dirty, but he went ahead and shook her hand saying, "The dirtier they are the more honoured I am. It is wonderful work you are doing here." I cannot forget that scene.

'There was so much disease, so much suffering among those refugees. Mother decided she must have a place where the very sick would be tended. She was looking for some land and at last she found it in a beautiful fruit garden. She called it Green Park. We had spent the day talking and talking to the man who owned it and now, as we prepared to leave, his wife brought us some cold drinks, just fresh lime juice. We were hot and tired but Mother said, "Our Congregation rules forbid us eating outside." The man said, "Mother, I am not asking you to eat, I'm only asking you to drink." So she took the glass and sipped from it. That was the first thing that had touched her lips that day – it was eleven o'clock at night.

'That land came just in time. Only the previous day a telegram had arrived advising us that a plane was bringing in a fully equipped hospital. All we needed was land on which to erect it. The plane arrived the next day.'

It was almost eight, but it was still light enough to see the city in blue and violet silhouette through the open doors. We asked Michael Gomes if we could go up to the terrace and we stumbled behind him up a dark, winding stairway and on to the roof contained by a balustrade still scarred by the outlines of bathing cubicles. Michael Gomes's grandchildren were flying kites, the paper squares wheeling crazily against the high, twilight sky. He began pointing out the landmarks : the steeples of St James's, St Teresa's and the Baithakhana Church; the distant steel towers of the Howrah Bridge with their lights glowing red; the dark sprawl of the city pierced by the shafts of high-rise buildings, slender minarets and the spires of temples. There was the sound of bells tamped by the distant drawl of traffic and a smell peculiar to Calcutta's long summer evenings. Incense. Smoke. Dust.

Pointing towards the steeples of the Baithakhana Church, Michael Gomes told us quite calmly that he helps in a school there, a school for problem children. 'It's called the Protima Sen School. We take those who are expelled and those whose families can no longer control them. One father came to me and said, "My son is a real delinquent. Will you take him?" I said, "Yes, provided he is a problem child." And there was the little boy who was caught red-handed stealing in someone's house. He had been pushed in through a small window by a gang of thieves who had trained him and who waited outside. He was handed over to the police who cajoled, praised, and tempted him to try and discover who he worked for. He was a little fellow and very frail, but he refused to say anything. The Police Commissioner who brought him to me said he was a marvellous little chap. He admired him. It seems he belonged to the

Moti Jheel slums. He used to stay on the "rocks".

'One day, some men came along and asked what he was doing there and why wasn't he in school. He said his father wouldn't send him to one, so they invited him to go with them, promising to put him into a school. And they did. It was a school for pick-pockets. There they gave him regular training. His sparse frame was just right for squeezing through barred windows or through small skylights. He was put into tram-cars because picking pockets in the crowded cars was considered comparatively easy. He was caught and the public gave him a terrible beating. The gang always had someone watching him so when he was brought back he was beaten again and his training continued. He was caught and stood trial several times, but he never gave the gang away. He came to us in 1968 and he's a respectable young man now, a wonderful character.

'We have to pay our teachers and we also have college students who give us two to three hours a week voluntarily. You know, we have a dancing teacher. He's a classical Manipuri dancer, a wonderful man. Mother was not happy about this and would not agree to my taking him on. She reasoned that we have school for only half a day, so how to teach dancing on top of that?

'On Mother's Feast Day, on 7 October, we held a special function and every one of her schools – she has many – gave one or two items. Whilst our school was performing, Mother said to me, "Michael, this is beautiful, it's a sin not to develop talents." I admitted to Mother that I had committed a sin. "You didn't agree to that dancing teacher being kept; well, I disobeyed you." She laughed. That's Mother, she's an eminently practical person. She makes rules and breaks rules. That's her strength.

'One day, while we were talking in the courtyard of the Mother House, the bell rang and Mother herself opened the door. There was a man outside and he was very hungry he said. "I've told you repeatedly to go to our Children's Home next door," Mother said, "that's the place where we feed people." But the man just stood there looking at Mother and then he said very quietly that he had eaten nothing for the last two days. There is a strict rule that the Sisters are not allowed to give anything from the Mother House, not even food, but Mother just went to the kitchen, brought a plateful of food and gave it to the man. He asked if he should empty it into a cloth and take it away or should he finish it there and give back the plate. "Take the plate and all," said Mother. The door-keeper, Sister Antonia, was surprised out of her wits, but Mother just laughed. Later Sister Antonia came and told me. "Do you know what she has done? Two Sisters have not yet come in for their meal. Their food was lying on the table and Mother just put one plate on top of the other and gave it to that man. Those two Sisters will have nothing to eat. There is nothing else."'

I thought aloud that the Sisters who live with Mother's impetuous behaviour must be rather wonderful people themselves and prepared for anything. 'Oh yes,' said Michael Gomes, 'I shall never forget a remark made by a Sister when she became a Missionary of Charity. They have to cut off their hair, you know, and that morning, after she had had her hair shorn, she said to me, "Do you know what happened? I felt as if Jesus was playing with my curls." When I asked her why, she said it was only the breeze.

'Then there was the day that Sister Andreas got a gold medal in her MBBS exam. She came back to the

Mother House very happily and showed it to Mother. "Well, Sister," asked Mother, "what will you do with it?" And Sister Andreas replied, "I didn't think of that." Mother said, "You must think. You don't need it. It is meaningless. You're not going into practice; you won't write MBBS (Gold Medallist) after your name. You'll be working among the poor, and what use will your gold medal be to them? Let someone else have it. Go and tell them you don't want it." So Sister Andreas went off happily and surrendered the medal. The boy who came second in the exam got it. He hangs it in his chamber.

'And I remember over here there was a Sister who, when she joined, couldn't speak English very well. One day, Mother was cleaning the toilet – there are no such things as servants among the Missionaries of Charity – and she just turned to the young Sister and said, "Go and get some ash." And she waited and waited and waited and then called, "Where have you gone, Sister?" The Sister came hurrying and Mother asked why she had taken so long. "Where's the ash?" "Ash, Mother? What ash? I thought you told me to have a wash. I had a bath this morning, but I've had another bath just now." Mother was very amused. That young nun has become a very wonderful person today.'

There are many who wonder, as I do, what will become of the Missionaries of Charity when Mother Teresa is no longer with them, for hers is the inspiration, the courage, the strength and the direction. Michael Gomes answered this question for me when he said, 'There are so many wonderful Sisters. One day Mother Teresa said to me, "You know, Michael, my main work is not all this. My concern is my Sisters. If they don't have the right spirit and the right approach then all our work is in vain." '

6. The Child that could not Cry

I cannot remember now who first told me about the child that could not cry, but I do remember visiting one of those multi-storied tenement houses in which anything up to eighty families occupy as many small rooms. The architect, if there had been one, had forgotten the kitchens so that every family cooked either on the narrow verandah or in their single room. An indelible impression of smoke, grey walls and sooty cobwebs remains. Coughing. An acrid stench. The child that could not cry, not more than eight months old, shared a small room with five other young children; the eldest of them, a girl of fourteen, was in charge. There was no fire here because there was no food to cook. The younger children huddled together in wide-eyed fear, the child that could not cry lay on a bed of sorts staring blankly at the ceiling, and the girl, called Rita, tall, slim, pretty, unafraid, talked to me.

Their father had disappeared some months before, leaving nothing. Somehow their mother had kept them from starving. Then, easily perhaps because she was so undernourished, she sickened and suddenly died. For a whole day they had not known what to do with her body. The neighbours had it removed. They had been kind, they had helped, but they too were poor and could not go on helping. Besides, there was the rent to pay. There was a man downstairs somewhere who had suggested that in return for looking after him he would pay the rent and feed her brothers and sisters. Young though she was, she was old enough to understand what that meant and, besides, she didn't want to leave her family for a moment, particularly the youngest who had stopped moving or making a sound. He did not even cry. Her great fear was that they would be separated, that the child would die. She would work, she would do anything as long as they could stay together.

When my story about the boy who could not cry appeared in the *Statesman*, the newspaper for which I work, the response was hearteningly quick. Money and offers to help poured in and there was a telephone call from Mother Teresa. In typical fashion she was prepared to take on the burden of the whole family. The older children could go to one of her schools and the young ones to her Home for abandoned children – Shishu Bhavan. I pointed out that Rita, the eldest girl, refused to be parted from the others. In that case, suggested Mother Teresa very practically, she would send a couple of Sisters to help Rita to cook for and nurse her young family until other arrangements could be made. When I said we had collected some seven thousand rupees, Mother came back pat with the suggestion that five thousand rupees could be put into a bank as Rita's dowry and the rest used to help the children. She explained that if Rita was to look forward to a happy, normal life, she should have a dowry. My immediate reaction was indignation that money so urgently required should be squandered on something I've no time for and have campaigned against. Mother obviously understood my misgivings because she took pains to tell me how necessary a dowry was for girls like Rita; without one she might never find a husband and, perhaps, be driven to prostitution and on to the streets. Mother's Indianness never ceases to amaze me.

Rita graduated from one of Mother's schools to a happy marriage and the children found love and care with the Sisters. The child who could not cry not only found his voice but well-to-do foster parents via Mother Teresa's Shishu Bhavan.

Shishu Bhavan is a nondescript two-storied building with a large courtyard that might once have been a garden but is now a concrete square dominated by the house and flanked by a kitchen, a dispensary and a small office. Entrance is usually not through the large green gate which is opened only to allow in goods-carrying trucks and ambulances, but through a small door in a high wall which, like the Mother House, has a chain and bell as its 'open sesame'. Immediately inside is a small grotto which offers shaded seats to the sick, hungry and weary, and a sense of compassion if they care to notice a rather beautiful statue of the Madonna.

There is always activity in Shishu Bhavan. Outside is the slow despairing shuffle of people queuing to be fed. Immediately inside is the large-scale cooking of food for the multitude and a seemingly unending dispensing of medicines for the sick. There are children everywhere, in the courtyard, on the stairs, on the landings and in the many rooms of the main building, because Shishu Bhavan is not just a home for abandoned children—though that is its main function. It is the work centre of the Missionaries of Charity, quite different from the cloistered serenity of the Mother House, and it is at Shishu Bhavan that the starving are fed and the ailing attended to. For those aware of the humble beginnings of Mother's mission, there is wondrous satisfaction to be derived from the fact that Shishu Bhavan stands not far from Creek Lane and the hospital outside which Mother Teresa picked up her first dying destitute.

The tragedy of being abandoned, homeless and unloved should pervade Shishu Bhavan, but it doesn't. There is a corner where unbelievably tiny infants are cared for, sometimes two or three to a cot, and often attached, as if still by their umbilical cords, to intravenous drip-feeders. There are infants picked up from the pavements, left on doorsteps or outside police posts, in drains or in refuse dumps. More recently, they have come also from city hospitals where Mother Teresa has left a standing request that all unwanted babies be handed over to her. 'I'm fighting abortion with adoption,' she says. I once had occasion to visit Shishu Bhavan on two consecutive days and on the second day missed several wizened faces I remembered from the day before. I asked a Sister attending where they were. She said they had died; they had not had a chance really. So many of them died, but it was better that they did here, where they were cared for and where love battled to keep them alive.

'Sometimes we get three or more babies a day,' said Sister Agnes. 'Always one for sure. More than half the number die because they are premature. I think some mothers have taken drugs to get rid of the children which harm them; they are drugged and need a great deal of care. Still they struggle to live and some are able to survive. If they do, it is a miracle. Some weigh less than two pounds, they are unable to suck and must be fed through the nose or by injection until they are strong enough to suck.'

Just a few cots removed from these hopelessly small children are rows of fortunate babies who have survived the shock of being unwanted, of attempted abortion, of premature birth. Once when Mother was taking us around she stopped by the cradle of a plump, gurgling child and said with a radiant smile, 'So you're going to be a little French boy, eh?' and then turning to us she explained that he had been adopted by a well-to-do French couple and would soon be flying out to join them.

'The French are wonderful,' said Sister Agnes. 'They sometimes take babies who cannot walk properly, their legs are not right. They write and say we have the ways and means, we will make it all right. They are not worrying whether the child is beautiful or not. They are not choosing. "We want to do something for the child," they say. They are so kind. This is charity, pure charity.'

Pure charity has its critics and opponents. I remember years ago Mother telling me, in some despair, that her scheme for adoptions outside India had been stopped. Somebody had accused her of selling Indian children; cases of 'nun-running' had been making headlines. She produced a large photograph album which quite obviously was an object of great love and asked me to look at it. There were photographs, many in colour, of children of all sizes and ages, under cowboy hats and pointing toy pistols in America, tobogganing in Switzerland, riding in England, celebrating a tree-filled Christmas in a German home and motoring with their new, very proud parents in France. Mother pointed to the photographs, naming names and places and saying, 'See how happy they are. So much love and so much beauty, and it's being stopped, eh.' In time, the ban was lifted which was why we could once again be introduced to a child who, abandoned on a Calcutta street, was going to people who wanted him in France.

'Yes, we have lots of adoptions in India, too,' said Sister Agnes. 'Recently, a couple came to ask for a baby. A very rich Hindu couple. They have wealth but no child. They come and say, "Sister, we want to take a baby. We have been married many years and have no baby." Then the husband tells me that his parents and brothers and all would look down on his wife because she has no child. They have an understanding; they tell his family that she is expecting a baby, then they come to us and say they want a newborn baby. Then they go on holiday and straight into a nursing home. And we give them a new-born baby. They're very happy. It's very beautiful, we appreciate it. We have helped many like that because we are very happy when a husband is willing to do that much to keep his wife despite his parents' objections. The husband and wife are very united but the husband's parents say "We have so much property and you have no children to leave it to; you have to marry a second time". But the husband is good and doesn't want to remarry and desert his wife. So they plan and take a baby. Of course,' said Sister Agnes with genuine innocence, 'they don't want anyone to know.'

I suspect that Sister Agnes, like many other Missionaries of Charity, has a special place in her heart for Shishu Bhavan. And understandably so. It's impossible to resist. The children come at you inviting affection, tugging at your clothes, holding your hand, asking for a piggyback, to be tossed in the air or swung around, smiling dribbly smiles and making baby noises. Some have sores – 'Heat,' says a Sister; some have shaven heads – 'Lice,' says a Sister; that one is terribly thin – 'Rickets,' says a Sister; that one looks hugely happy – 'She's mentally deficient,' said a Sister.

I've come across some beautiful children at Shishu Bhavan who were retarded : twin Chinese boys, handsome and strongly built, for whom apparently there was no hope; they had to be tied up when they became violent. And there was the little girl who loved Mother Teresa with a frenzy and would hold on to her hand and keep jumping up and down spilling laughter. Mother told me sadly that she was a hopeless case, like so many others for whom she would like to have a home. And there was a young boy from Darjeeling who wouldn't speak and resisted everyone. He harboured a dreadful, deep sorrow in his eyes which suggested that he had been witness to some terrible experience. I tried to speak to him in Nepalese without effect, then brought a young Tibetan photographer to try and break through in Tibetan. That didn't work either: he sat huddled and withdrawn, weighed down with sadness. I heard later that he had been ill-treated by relatives with whom he had been left by his parents. When the boy responded with silence and a refusal to eat and was in danger of dying, he was handed over to the Missionaries of Charity in Darjeeling who had sent him to Calcutta. It was through the Tibetan photographer that the boy was eventually reunited with his parents.

The same young photographer was involved in a happier incident at Shishu Bhavan. We were on a visit with Mother Teresa watching food and medicine being loaded into army trucks for the refugees from Bangladesh who were then pouring into Calcutta. Mother, diminutive beside a tall army major and his lanky men, was very much in command of the situation. It was amusing watching her order them into action, they obeying her with smart salutes. I wanted a photograph, but there was not a sign of my friend, the photographer. When Mother noticed me searching for something she said casually, 'Your friend is probably upstairs photographing our very pretty German nun.' True enough, he was.

'We had a boy whose parents were dead and whose grandmother was very old,' said Sister Agnes. 'She came to Mother and said that as she could die any time, she wanted Mother to have the boy. So we took him into Shishu Bhavan. He finished his School Final exam and studied a little more; by this time he was with the Brothers in Howrah. When he was small, whenever Mother used to ask him what he was going to do when he grew up, he used to say, "I will become Mother Teresa." So Mother put him in a Seminary and he became a priest.

'Many of our children are happily married. There was a boy, Sukomal. One day, Mother found him sitting under a tree. He'd lost his parents and was staying with his uncle and aunt who used to make him work, work, work and not give him enough to eat. So he ran away and was begging and stealing when Mother found him. So Mother brought him to Shishu Bhavan. He studied and went to technical school and is now working. Mother didn't want him to get married so early, but there is something so sad, so lonely about these total orphans you cannot blame them for wanting someone. When Mother asked him why he was in such a hurry to get married, he replied, "How long can I stay like this? I have nobody to call my own." So two of us went to his village for his wedding because he had to have somebody from his family to stand for him. I bought him his clothes and gave him everything for his wife. Mother has also bought him a plot of land and he's building a house. They will stay with the girl's parents till it is ready.

'We had a girl called Sadhana. When she was very

young her mother died and her father married again.
Her stepmother who didn't want her was always scold-
ing her and beating her. One day, she heard her stepmother tell her father that he must decide who he
wanted – her or Sadhana. Shortly afterwards her father,
saying that he was taking her out shopping, took Sadhana to the railway station and left her there. She stayed
there all day and night, terrified and crying, waiting for
him to return, but he never did. We took her to Shishu
Bhavan and when she was old enough we gave her in
marriage to a nice young man. As a dowry Mother gave
her a little land and a little house. They are very happy
and have four or five children. Then, very sad, her
husband got TB. So we are trying to get her some work.
She is our child. She has no mother to go to. There is
no end to the sufferings of our people.

'Among the people we feed at Shishu Bhavan are the
breadwinners of large families. They are working but they
are terribly poor. Take a father who earns one hundred
rupees (£5) a month. Thirty rupees (£1.50) goes on
rent, so they cannot eat for at least one week a month,
and even then there is very little. Often, they cannot
afford to draw their rations regularly so they forfeit
their ration cards which allow them to buy staples
cheaply. It is terrible, and we can do mighty little.

'We are supposed to do only for the poorest of the
poor. We cannot help the millions of ordinary poor
though their need is really great. In Calcutta, there is
so much wealth but the poor are so badly treated. Very
often people come to us and ask for someone – a servant
– for a job. I get very annoyed with them because they
are asking one poor person to do as much as two or
three people. When I enquire how much they are
willing to pay – because our poor cannot ask – they avoid

the question. I always ask them because I know what they think : "Just because Sister is giving us this poor woman she can be treated any way." That will not do. They sometimes say, forty rupees (£2) or fifty rupees (£2.50), and I ask, "Would you work for that?" At least they must be able to feed themselves; they must not starve when they are working. So nowadays few come here for servants. Those who want cheap labour go elsewhere. I tell you, the poor are unjustly treated and unjustly paid. Some people will not give a man working for only sixty rupees (£3) a month any rest. They make him work, work, work. And still he cannot feed his family properly. It is very pathetic.

'People come and tell me, "Sister, the days are very hard, we cannot afford to give a servant much." I tell them, "You cannot keep a servant then. Very hard days for you are very hard days for them. You can't make a person do as much as you want. You don't say anything about working times, and they cannot complain." They cause our poor to faint and blame hard days.

'We do find employment for our poor. Our women could go and look after children. We try and get them at least one or two meals a day and sixty rupees (£3) a month. To employ them without meals is not fair. Yet, some women get only thirty (£1.50) or forty (£2) rupees and they and their families are on the footpaths starving. It is simply terrible. We are trying to help them; we try to give them a meal. So we are trying to feed them at Shishu Bhavan.

'There's so much unemployment in the country. People with qualifications, people with degrees even. You cannot understand what is the situation of these people. Though they are very poor they make an effort nowadays to study everything. But when they finish, even

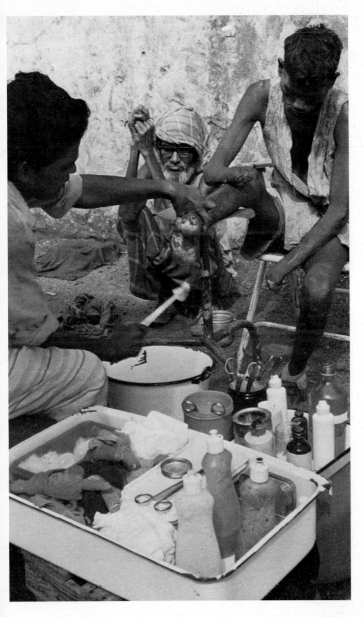

She sought, and got, permission to start a Congregation of
Brothers and began encouraging men into the Order

'Mother decided she must have a place where the very sick would be tended'

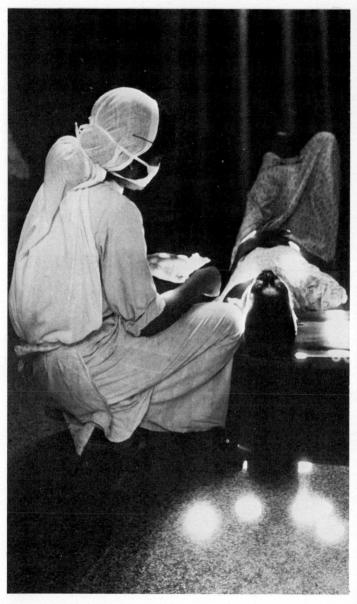

Nobody in Nirmal Hriday has died depressed, in despair,
unwanted, unfed or unloved

with credits, they will not get jobs because they do not have the influence or the money to bribe. But the boy with no credits but with the means will get the job. What does a young person feel when all his effort has come to nothing?

'Nowadays you cannot blame anyone for not working. The main need is to create employment. We are working for people, Mother says, who cannot run in the mad rush for development. We have to look after them. For one family that is coming up there are ten families going down. For one businessman coming up so many poor are crushed. That is very pathetic. Afterwards, of course, these young boys who cannot get employment become loafers and after that you cannot make them work. Because in the beginning nobody cared, nobody bothered, they get used to loitering, stealing and drinking and their young lives are spoilt.

'Many people help us but they can do more than that. They give donations but they should not feel that their duty is over. Our people are suffering and it is our duty, not just charity, to help them. Just giving money won't work. If only the poor worker was paid better, they wouldn't have to come to us for help.

'We sponsor children. Say, a widow has five or six children; we sponsor one or two – the bright ones – so at least they will be able to help the family when they grow up. We see them through school and give them some vocational training. We do not help in college education because it has no meaning nowadays. Look at the areas in which these children live; no light to study, not enough food to eat, no space to play in; they never see meat or fish, just rice and lentils and salt, and they are expected to educate themselves like that.

'Sometimes now we are having three meals a day and

M.T. – D

when we miss one we feel hungry. The poor people do not even have one meal. How much torture they are going through. So many of them die. Our Home in Kalighat is for people in the last stages. They often leave children behind them and they come to Shishu Bhavan. Very often the babies die an hour or a day later, but Mother says, "I don't care what people say about the death rate. Even if they die an hour later, let them come, the babies must not die uncared for and unloved. Because even a baby can feel. If we refuse them then we are closing our doors and these babies will be killed. It is better they die a natural death in their time than be killed." '

7. A Gift of Love

In the parlour of the Mother House of the Missionaries of Charity hang three boards. On one is displayed the four vows that the Society takes in pursuing 'Jesus's Way of Life'. The vows are poverty, chastity, obedience and charity. Another board, illustrated by photographs, explains what is required of the Congregation as they walk 'In the Footsteps of Christ'. The photographs show the Sisters at work in the slums, in homes for the abandoned and dying destitutes, in schools, among lepers and in mobile dispensaries. Inscribed above and below the photographs are Mother Teresa's own prayers, 'Make us worthy, Lord, to serve our fellow-men through the world who live and die in poverty and hunger. Give them, through our hands, this day their daily bread, and, by our understanding, love, peace and joy.'

'Let each Sister see Jesus Christ in the person of the poor; the more repugnant the work or the person, the greater also must be her faith, love and cheerful devotion in ministering to our Lord in this distressing disguise.'

The third board outlines the structure of the Society, founded in 1950 by Mother Teresa. Its idea is 'To quench the thirst of Jesus Christ on the Cross for love of souls by the Sisters' observance of the four vows of poverty, chastity, obedience and charity'. It attempts to tell at a glance how many Aspirants, Postulants and

Professed Sisters there are, and to give in some detail
the places in India and abroad where branch Houses
of the Missionaries of Charity have been established,
together with the dates of their founding. So numerous
and urgent are the calls on the Missionaries of Charity,
and so fast does the Order expand that this board can
never hope to be up-to-date.

When Mother observed us copying down the figures
from the board, she warned us that they were not
correct, so we asked Sister Agnes if she could help us
with the latest statistics. She did, but even as we read
them, press reports on the opening of yet another Home
for dying destitutes in the once princely city of Hydera-
bad made the latest list obsolete. The report went on
to say that Mother would be visiting the cities of
Bombay and Poona before returning to Calcutta via
Patna where unprecedented floods had almost submerged the city causing loss of life and untold hardship.

Quoting at random from Sister Agnes's impressive
list of statistics, the Missionaries of Charity have sixty-
one foundations in India (fifty-one manned by Sisters
and ten by Brothers) and twenty-eight abroad. They have
eighty-one schools, three hundred and thirty-five mobile
dispensaries, twenty-eight family planning centres, sixty-
seven leprosy clinics, twenty-eight Homes for abandoned
children and thirty-two Homes for dying destitutes. The
Order has some nine hundred and thirty-five Sisters and
one hundred and eighty-five Brothers. Sister Agnes puts
the number of patients treated by the mobile dispensaries at about one million six hundred thousand, and
the number of inmates at present in Homes for dying
destitutes at two thousand, against which is a note explaining that the numbers of admissions and deaths

have been omitted. Over forty-three thousand lepers are being treated at the leprosy clinics and the Missionaries of Charity are, at this moment, taking care of nearly two thousand abandoned children. Not mentioned are the millions of starving people who have been, and are being, fed by the Missionaries of Charity every day. I doubt that the good Sisters could count the numbers themselves.

Mother Teresa explains that she came to India because it was a mission country, but then happily adds that Indian missionaries are now to be found on all five continents, even in the most affluent countries of the West. 'In England, they suffer from loneliness. They have no need for bread, but they need human love. That is the hungry Christ for us.' She told us of old people dying alone in their often well-to-do homes and their bodies being found days afterwards. 'In the Yemen, the Sisters are called "carriers of God's love". It's wonderful, eh? There is now a church, a tabernacle, in the Yemen after eight hundred years. A person there told me that the presence of the Sisters has breathed a new life into the people.'

Father Henry recalls how one of the Sisters working among the Arabs in Jerusalem once asked the British Representative's wife for overcoats. 'So now the lady asks in great surprise, "Overcoats?" And the Sister replies, "Yes, they will make excellent mattresses." Those Sisters in Jerusalem had to go from Jews to Arabs, Arabs to Jews. One day some Arabs said, "These are to be shot." The Missionaries of Charity calmly prepared to die. Then the Arabs realized they were going to make a blunder and they said, "Not these ones. Though they go and come they do not carry cameras and tape-

recorders. These are helping the poor. They are angels." '
And Father Henry added, 'Theirs was an infiltration of
love.'

'In Australia,' said Sister Agnes, 'we are working
among the aborigines and among the alcoholics and
drug addicts. Imagine, we have to keep drink in our
House. It is necessary. One old man who was trying
very hard to give up drinking was suddenly moved to
drink and he said to me, "Sister, you come along with
me to the bar and you wait outside while I have one.
Just one. Promise." If you want to save someone, you
have to have patience. You know, it's marvellous : we
girls from India, particularly Bengal, are very protected
and there we are working among alcoholics. In Rome,
our Sisters go to the Barracks, that's the slums. We have
a crèche there. In London, we work among the gipsies
and the other poor.'

In Africa, Mother Teresa explained, one is not allowed
to call the needy poor. 'The word "poor" has so many
meanings, but they are our people, our brothers and
sisters.' And then she told us how in Miami, where
her Missionaries of Charity visit gaols, the prisoners
voiced their appreciation of the Sisters by saying that they
'look and dress like women'.

Some years ago, when Mother Teresa met the Queen
of Bhutan, she was disturbed to hear that there was a
large incidence of leprosy in the northern valleys of the
beautiful Himalayan kingdom. Apparently, it was the
practice in the Tibet of old to drive lepers out of the
country and many of them found refuge in the high
empty valleys of Bhutan. Mother was eager to begin
work among these lepers and I believe the Queen extended her an invitation to visit Bhutan and ascertain
if something could be done. Somehow the plan fell

through. It could have been Mother's insistence on certain conditions being met before she starts a mission in any place, whether in India or abroad. 'Our first consideration is that there are the kind of people who need our help. And it is very important that we have a priest with us. We cannot do without Holy Communion every day. That would mean being without Christ.' Even when the Pope invited her to work in the slums of Rome, she gave the request earnest consideration and then went to see things for herself before agreeing. Finally, as Mother so often stresses, there must be the conviction that what she is doing, no matter where it is or what it is, is God's work.

In April 1973, ICI (India) gave a large modern build-ing that had been built as the Company's central labora-tories, together with ample grounds, to Mother Teresa. To her, it was a wonderful example of 'Love in Action', and she appropriately called the place, Prem Daan which, translated literally, means 'Gift of Love'.

The gift is yet so fresh that Mother Teresa has not had time to adapt it to her final needs, but already its vast halls, its galleries, its corridors and offices are filled with Mother's people, the very sick in mind and body.

The guard at the entrance is a Nepalese who was cured of advanced tuberculosis at one of Mother's clinics and never tires of saying, with considerable emotion, how happy he is to be working for her. As we entered the building we were met by a quite distinguished-looking Anglo-Indian gentleman who had once owned a small engineering company and racehorses. He held us fas-cinated in conversation about old people and old times. He was sure he had met me before : at the races? At a party? Or was it at some diplomatic reception? Noting our bewilderment – he wore a striped pyjama suit and obviously belonged – Mother discreetly signalled that he was touched. He followed us for a while asking if we had met his lost son, then turned disconsolately away leaving me to wonder where we might have met before.

The large halls that gave one into the other were packed with low beds and every one of them was occupied. Too weak almost to move, many of the patients raised their hands in greeting or smiled as we passed. Others followed us with their eyes. There is a rare quality in Mother Teresa's Homes that has been described as miraculous and can be argued as either a deep sense of anaesthetizing shock or the beauty of acceptance and absolute tranquillity. I have seen no auras, no miraculous illumination, but I have felt a depth of trusting innocence and peace in these receptacles of human despair and degradation that I have met nowhere else.

We were accompanied that day by Sir William and Lady Collins, fresh from the clean air and mountains of Bhutan. It would have been understandable if they had been repulsed or had expressed a word or look of horror. On the contrary, they were deeply moved by the wonder of their experience, returning smiles and greetings and talking across the barriers of language with sympathy.

There were two young people in those cavernous halls that day who were helping the Sisters clean and feed and comfort. One was a French girl who was going from one desperately ill person to another, tenderly feeding and encouraging them in the only language she knew, and they somehow understood. Their smiles said so. The other was a young American who was plainly radiating God's love. He spoke in ecstasy and there was the kind of glow in his eyes that one reads about. He was administering to the particularly wretched cases with a tenderness other men his age use to express their first breathless outpourings of love. He was from New York, a Jew; he had travelled all over but, man, he had never seen anything like this. So beautiful, so beautiful.

There is a large room in Prem Daan where the demented are cared for; it is one of the few institutions in Calcutta for the mad. As we entered the room, a woman near the door began wailing hysterically and several other inmates started calling out loudly to Mother. Here, surely, I thought, even with their boundless compassion, it must be particularly difficult for the Sisters to penetrate the fog of depression, fear, despair and anxiety. Lending substance to my thoughts was a young girl who paced up and down a barred cubicle at the far end of the room like a caged animal. The sight of us seemed to agitate her, so that, suddenly, she climbed on a bed, reached towards a high skylight and began beating on the glass pane with her fists. Horror. Any moment the glass might splinter. Her hands tear, sever. I pointed out the danger to Mother. She quickly went to the cubicle, opened the door and pleaded with the girl to come down. For a while she stared defiantly then obeyed reluctantly, swinging slowly to the floor. Mother had rejoined us when the girl wrenched open the door and advanced upon us menacingly. I felt something ghastly was about to happen. Everyone hushed and I could sense a strange tension among the patients that might erupt into uncontrollable madness.

Very quietly, very composed, Mother Teresa walked towards the girl. It could have been the charged atmosphere which made me view what happened next in slow motion, like a significant sequence in a horror film. When the girl was within reach, Mother spread her arms as if in welcome and then clasped her by both shoulders speaking gently to her all the while. For a moment, it looked as if the girl might push Mother aside but instead she faltered and submissively allowed Mother, arm around her shoulders, to walk her back to her cell. The woman near the door began wailing again and the others returned to their restless movements and chatter.

Years ago in a cul-de-sac in a Howrah slum, Mother Teresa was attending to lepers when a frightened bull charged into the lane. An old gentleman who got into the way was knocked down and gored and it seemed that nothing could prevent the maddened animal from tossing into the terrified lepers. Mother Teresa stepped forward directly into the path of the bull and, according to the person who told me the story, stretched her arms wide. Perhaps the animal was alarmed by this unexpected apparition, or perhaps it instinctively knew that it had reached the end of the cul-de-sac. Whatever the explanation, it stopped and turned and walked quietly away.

As we were leaving Prem Daan, Raghu Rai and myself trailing behind the others taking photographs, there was a startling crash of glass and a human cry. A few feet from where I stood, frozen at the sight, a tormented someone wrapped in dirty sacking was reaching hands towards me through a shattered glass pane. At any moment those frail hands could be skewered on the large slivers of glass still embedded in the broken window. Raghu Rai stepped quickly forward and, in a voice wondrously persuasive, asked that whoever it was remove the dirty sacking from its head. He repeated the request several times, adding that the possessor of such beautiful hands must surely have a matchingly beautiful face. Dramatically, the cloth was unwound, very slowly, fumblingly, and there was a lovely face behind it – a young girl who looked at us with a troubled, shy smile. Then, with horrid determination, she reached her arms through the jagged glass towards us, splinters of broken glass clasped in clenched hands, offering them to us. Raghu, very gently, very patiently, begged her to drop the splinters saying that it was wrong for such lovely hands to hold such filthy things. For a long while she just looked at us with that strange, remote smile and then, one by one, she opened her hands and allowed the glass splinters to fall. Now Raghu begged her to step back into the room and, even as she hesitated, began removing the cruel shafts of glass from the window with his hands. She watched fascinated until he was done and then laughingly disappeared into the deep gloom of the room. I felt briefly chilly in the hot sun.

There was one more thing to see at Prem Daan, and that was Mother Teresa's small rehabilitation centre inside the gates. To this centre, the city's destitute bring empty green coconut shells that litter the city streets; fresh coconut milk is a popular cheap refreshment. At Prem Daan these coconuts are dried and processed and made into such profitable articles as coir mats, bags and rope. Mother Teresa calls the process 'changing garbage into gold'. In fact, it does more since it is estimated that hundreds of tons of green coconut shells each day are responsible for aggravating the problem of garbage removal in the city. So part of the city's waste provides gainful employment for a growing number of Mother Teresa's people. When this humble enough activity caught the attention of the Press, it was reported that Mother Teresa and her Missionaries of

Charity had taken on the responsibility of ridding Calcutta of its historic garbage problem. Many a city inhabitant must have wondered, even hoped.

On the other side of the city, near the busy Kidderpore docks, a group of Mother Teresa's nuns have started a self-help centre of another kind. 'I pray for paper,' said Sister Premila, a very forthright, articulate nun who has charge of a branch House of the Missionaries of Charity. 'It is a daughter house, I suppose,' she said. 'We are far too many now for the Mother House. We go out from here to work in Kidderpore where we have a malnutrition unit, a dispensary and a self-help centre. I started it, actually. Last May, when I was just professed, Mother told me to go and see what I could do for the people there. So I went around the slums for a few days to see what their need was and found a number of children just two or three years old who were unable to stand. They were just sitting around.

'I had done a physiotherapy course, so when I saw these children I thought I should start a centre for them. I soon found they were weak from malnutrition. Kidderpore being a dock area, people are employed only when the ships come in. When the ships go out they sit at home and starve with their families. So I thought I should do something for the women, and that's how I started the paper business. When I asked what they were capable of doing, they told me they used to make paper bags for sale, but when the price of waste paper became so much, it was impossible for them to carry on. They had to give up making bags.

'My idea was to supply them with a little paper. I began with one or two women and now I have about seventy-five to whom I give paper every day. They make the bags at home and earn about two or three rupees

(10 to 15 pence per day. They would be able to earn much more if I was able to provide paper. That's why I pray for paper.

'I beg around from anyone who looks as if they might have some paper. I've put up appeals in all the churches and parish halls and I went around the schools explaining my scheme to the Principals. I also go around offices. One day two of us Sisters were standing at a tram stop when, unknown to us, a lady secretary was wondering how to dispose of a lot of waste company paper. She had been instructed to get rid of it. Looking out of the window she saw us and made up her mind. We got a lot of paper from there.

'The bags our women make are bought by small grocers and street vendors. They are in great demand. The women who make them have no other skills : widows mostly, women who have been used to doing only domestic work, deserted by husbands. For women with skills, I have a home-craft unit where they do needlework and crochet and make some really beautiful things. I buy the thread and whatever else they need because they don't have any capital. They show me what they make before they sell it and if it is of very good quality I try and find a market for it. It's amazing how quickly our malnutrition cases improve when I help the family to earn some money.'

From the moment we entered the 'daughter house', through a large gate with the inevitable summoning bell, and found ourselves in a tiny hallway, I had begun wondering about Sister Premila. We had been advised to meet her by Sister Agnes and, without knowing why, had anticipated someone special. For an instant, as she walked hastily and soundlessly into the small room, I was disappointed. There was no aura of personality, no radiance of the kind that suffuses Mother's worn face. She was tall, slim, almost undernourished and plain, the way mannequins are plain without make-up. And apprehensive. Then she did something special. She offered us a glass of water on a tray apologizing that there was nothing else. It was a hot day and we obviously looked thirsty, but the tray and the apologies had me imagining a very different person to the one who sat demurely before us in a threadbare white cotton sari. The years of self-imposed poverty, privation and selflessness had not completely exorcized the past. Quite obviously, Sister Premila was not one of the schoolgirls Mother Teresa had inspired to follow her into the wilderness. Here was someone who had renounced the everyday pleasures of life in the fullness of living.

'I don't know if you can understand when I say it is Christ who makes me what I am. So much depends on one's relationship with God. As Mother says, He was naked and He was thirsty, but there is no use regretting that I was not alive at the time when Jesus was living. You see, He is alive for me here. It does not come into the picture that if only I had lived then I would have followed Him. Of course I would have. But He is here for me today no matter what I could have done, so it does not make any difference where I am sent or what I do.

'After I had made my profession, Mother told me to go to Kidderpore and do something. There wasn't a House there, she didn't give me any place to stay. She didn't suggest what I should do or where I should go, like start a dispensary or something : it would have been easy if she had. Then she went off abroad and didn't come back for months. When she returned I asked her if she didn't want to see what I was doing or even know about it and she said yes, she would. I don't know what she expected. She had only said I must do something for the poor. She saw what I was doing in Kidderpore just a short while ago.'

Sister Premila has been with the Missionaries of Charity for about ten years. She is a trained school-teacher and, of her own admission, wanted to teach in 'the best of schools because they give you the best money and have the best students. A job satisfaction too.' She was born in Mangalore, in South India, a lovely, leisurely place where poverty is gentle and not obvious. In Bombay, where she went to teach, things were very different. 'I had never seen anybody take anyone off the streets. There are so many people on the streets in Bombay. I hadn't been to Calcutta then. I found I had a great desire to do something, but I didn't know what, until I visited a school run by Mother Teresa and I was taken aback. It was in the heart of a slum and because it was the rainy season the whole place was flooded. The houses were just three feet square, made with four poles and rags and things, and whole families were living in them. Right in the middle of the slum they had built a school, exactly like the structures people were living in, only a little bigger. There were a hundred children and the Sisters were not qualified teachers. One told me she had not even passed her Matric. But she had done her best with gunny-sacks and charcoal drawings on some bits of paper straight on the walls.

'I was deeply moved because in our proper schools we are so fastidious about equipment and surroundings. I thought, here I was a qualified teacher, doing what? You know, it does not remain only to help. It requires more.

'At first, though Mother was so famous, I had not heard of her until just three months before I joined her. I heard it mentioned, very casually, that a nun was picking up people from the streets. I went along because I had never seen such a thing before. Mother was on a visit to Bombay and when I met her I wanted to become a volunteer but she asked me if I would not like to join her. For ever. And I did.'

We went to visit Sister Premila at her work centre in Kidderpore. Ekbalpore Road, where the centre is located in a presbytery, has known better days. Well-to-do Anglo-Indians who had made their money in shipping had built houses there (one straight out of London suburbia) and it is easy to imagine them building their dreams there too, of an Anglo-Indian enclave with its own school and church and club and atmosphere of the 'Old Country'. The Anglo-Indians have departed, but we met one at the Presbytery of St Ignatius, a well-built, grey-haired friendly person, who introduced himself simply as Uncle. He had once been a sailor and was tempted, as we looked around the building with its few remaining pieces of period furniture, to talk of the old days, wandering days, wooing days, fun and dancing days. It was easy to see Uncle as the spirit of the parish parties. But, if he was eager to forget the present with the past, he was very concerned with the part Mother Teresa and her Congregation played in it. 'I tell you, they're doing wonderful things. I tell you, this woman is a saint, a walking, living saint.' It was Uncle who took us behind the building to a small yard where some Sisters and Brothers were conducting a dispensary and food kitchen, and Sister Premila a sewing class. About twenty women, Hindu and Muslim, sat in a circle on the floor chatting happily while they cross-stitched, embroidered, crocheted attractive things like table sets, guest towels, duchesse sets and handbags. There was a queue of elderly, less well-dressed women waiting for Sister Premila to give them paper, and beyond them were other women, visibly pregnant, awaiting medical attention. Among all these women was a grey-bearded old Muslim with a small pot-bellied child which he kept caressing with devotion touching to see. He surprised me by saying the child was his son : he could have been its great-grandfather. His wife had died in childbirth and now he, too old to work, and his son were living on a pavement, dependent on the Missionaries of Charity for all their needs. It was he who told us about the miracle. His child had died; there was no doubt that it was dead; he was the father, wasn't he? He knew. In grief, he had brought the body to Sister Premila. Pointing at the unsuspecting nun he said with a tremulous voice, 'It was she. She made him live. She made him walk. See, he can walk,' and he launched the child into a halting run by pushing it gently.

Inside the small dispensary, there was another miracle in the making. An unbelievably small, wizened child, it looked premature, was being loved into living by a young French girl who was then a co-worker with the Missionaries of Charity. With infinite care she inserted a needle that seemed out of all proportion to the child's body into its arm and adjusted the drip-feed. She was far too busy to talk, but Sister Premila told us that she was a trained nurse on holiday in India who spoke nothing but French. We heard only weeks later that she had received permission to remain in India and join the Missionaries of Charity. And we had an opportunity to see her later in the humble white sari of the Order, at a service we attended in the Mother House.

Four Brothers, all remarkably young, were doctoring and feeding a swarm of lepers on the street outside the presbytery. They might have been organizing a Sunday School picnic, they were so cheerful, so casual, dressed in ordinary shirts and trousers and wearing slippers. Unlike the Sisters of the Order, the Brothers have no particular uniform.

The Brother House is just around the corner from the presbytery of St Ignatius, an undistinguished three-storied concrete building which with its barred windows, wooden shutters and cast-iron verandah railing looks like any of its neighbours. No pretensions here to Anglo-India and the 'Home Country'. No faded dreams and shabby elegance. The parlour is a claustrophobically small room with green peeling walls made beautiful by a framed Hindi proverb :

> If you have
>   two loaves of bread
> Give one to the poor,
>   sell the other —
> And buy hyacinths
>   to feed your soul.

I had first visited this House some ten years ago when a group of Brothers were taking their vows. A colourful cloth canopy had been erected on the roof of the building and had been decorated with banana leaves and lotus blossoms in the traditional way of Bengal. So are houses decorated for marriages and festivals. Mother Teresa was there with a few Sisters. The Archbishop of Calcutta presided. There were joyous hymns sung in Hindi and Bengali, a heavy mist of incense and in that festive atmosphere the Sacrament seemed to gain in majesty and mystery. It was here that for the first time I realized how intense, how fervent, was Mother Teresa's passion for the Sacrament. I watched fascinated as her eyes followed the Eucharist with an almost hungry longing. When she knelt to receive it, she might have been kneeling at the feet of the Lord, there was such ecstasy on her face. I've heard her say since then, 'I cannot do without Mass and Holy Communion. Without Jesus. If I can see Jesus in the appearance of bread then I will be able to see Him in the broken bodies of the poor. That is why I need that oneness with Christ. If I have that deep faith in the Eucharist, naturally I will be able to touch Him in the broken bodies because He has said, "I am the Living Bread." '

At that ceremony I had met Brother Andrew, an Australian Jesuit who, like Mother Teresa, felt he had a vocation within a vocation, that even as a priest he was not doing enough to make his peace with God. In the words of Mother Teresa, 'I think for a long time he was working to give himself totally to the poor. He is a very holy person, really very holy. He was a very gifted Jesuit in every possible way, spiritually, mentally, physically. And both of us have the same mind. That is the most extraordinary thing. But we are so different. Naturally, he is much more gifted than I, very gifted. He was not the first Brother. The Brothers started in March 1963 and Brother Andrew started in 1965. It coincides very beautifully because the very day the work of the Brothers began here in Calcutta, on the twenty-fifth of March 1963, he was ordained a Jesuit priest in Hazaribagh, where the Australian Mission is. He just came to us for a while in 1964 to see what we were doing. After that there was no question of what he would do. He heard the call.'

Formerly Father Ian Travers-Ball, Brother Andrew is now the Superior of the Brothers of the Order. I remember him as tall, almost painfully thin; a warm, frank person with a smile that puts one immediately at ease. Unfortunately, I never got to know him. One knew he was there working silently away in some desperate area of need, organizing the small but growing band of Brothers and establishing Brother Houses all over the country. Then he was gone. When we tried to search him out he was in Viet Nam and Mother Teresa, though she tried not to show it, was anxious about him. Saigon, where he was last heard of, had been overrun. Though all foreigners were leaving Viet Nam, Brother Andrew had decided to stay.

So, it was Brother Ferdinand, the Assistant General of the Brothers, who received us in the small parlour of the Brother House. Brother Ferdinand is small but wiry and gives the impression of being austere, frugal, even severe. He is young, about thirty, and soft-spoken. He joined the Order in 1967 which was the year that Mother Teresa bought the House in Kidderpore. Until then the Brothers had been staying near the Mother House and going out with the Sisters to help them in their work. It was because Mother Teresa had felt that there was some work that could be done better by men that she sought, and got, permission to start a Congregation of Brothers and began encouraging men into the Order.

'I know little about the beginning,' said Brother Ferdinand. 'But, after we got this House, the number of Brothers increased rapidly. Unfortunately, in 1970, we lost many. You see, our way of life is rather poor and our work is hard. Many of the Brothers come from good families and so are used to a much better life than this. At the same time, we do not want to raise our standard of living. We work amongst the poorest of poor people so we must try to live as simply as they. We must practise poverty among ourselves. Our food is very simple, our clothes are very simple, and whatever we get we share. Our way of life is very hard for many young boys but by the grace of God our numbers are increasing.

'I feel God's call for me and it is a grand gift of God. Before coming here I worked in a coal-mine for six years. I had a good salary and everything, but I kept hearing about Mother Teresa's work in Calcutta and when my aunty came to join Mother Teresa she used to write to me very often. Naturally, I wanted to see what kind of person this is, why the whole world is speaking about her work. So I came to Calcutta to spend a month with the Brothers and on the very first day I met Mother. She spared me nearly twenty minutes and I knew I was in the proper place. It was really God calling me to be with Mother and work for her poor people.

'It's like this for the other Brothers too. They are inspired not only by Mother but by the wonderful work that the Society is doing. I cannot express myself more than by saying that it is a gift of God for us. And we really feel that God has called us to His special mission, to have His message spread to the down-trodden people. And when we think deeply about our service to the poor then we feel ourselves very close to God.'

The Brothers, now one hundred and seventy-five strong, with ten Houses in India and two in South Viet Nam, work in particularly tough localities tending the chronically ill, dying destitutes, lepers, juvenile delinquents, drug addicts and mental patients. When we met Brother Ferdinand, he made it clear that he was not yet professed but would be taking his final vows at St Ignatius's Church in a few weeks' time along with some other Brothers. Mother Teresa invited us along and once again I was witness to a touchingly simple service. There were no flowers or bunting this time, no colourful canopy and the electricity had failed so it was dark inside the church despite a brilliant summer sun outside. A small group of Brothers, two foreigners among them, made their solemn vows in the presence of relatives and friends and the carved saints who looked severely down from their niches in the aisle. I sat near a group of young Brothers still to take their vows, who formed the choir. The hymns, accompanied on harmoniums and Indian drums, were joyously beautiful.

After the service, in a happy, chattering confusion of greeting and congratulation that welled outside the church, we were introduced to Brother Aloysius by Mother Teresa. Brother Aloysius, a friendly smiling boy from South India, was surrounded by his family who had come to Calcutta especially for the occasion. The women wore the vivid silk saris of the South and held large bouquets of flowers. They had flowers in their hair; except for two, who wore the blue-bordered white saris of the Missionaries of Charity. Mother told us happily that the two nuns were Aloysius's sisters. There had once been a third, named Sister Aloysius. She died, so her brother, Martin, then studying in South India, decided to join the Missionaries of Charity and take his sister's name. There couldn't have been a happier, more satisfied family under the Indian sun that morning. Looking at them lovingly, and with a pride quite permissible on an occasion such as this, Mother Teresa said, 'It's wonderful, eh?'

8. The Place of the Pure Heart

Kalighat, on the banks of a brown, sacred stream in south Calcutta, is named after the ancient temple to Kali, a powerful Hindu goddess. It is one of the most congested areas in an overcrowded city. One of its oldest. A labyrinth of narrow lanes, middle-class boxes, slums, shops, pilgrims' rest-houses and *ghats* where the dead are cremated. The temple itself, built in the sugar-loaf style of medieval Bengal, reaches above the congestion like a flower for sunlight. Its precincts swarm. Rich and poor. A millionaire family bearing expensive gifts in gold tissue. Devotees in white cotton leading goats to sacrifice. Saffron-robed *yogis* with piled hair and extravagant caste marks vermilioned on their foreheads. Beggars. Tourists. Troubadours singing devotional songs, plaintive, like sighs set to music. Balloon-men almost airborne. Skeins of students. Mendicants. And now, strangely, nuns in blue-bordered white saris.

There is always a festive confusion about Kalighat, particularly in its shanty shops which sell everything from fruit and carved wood to brass cooking pots and images; from gaudy flowers and toys to religious prints, fresh fish and caged birds. Over all is the blue mist of funeral pyres, and the smell of incense mingles with the smell of death. Boisterous life and a calm acceptance of death is characteristic of Kalighat. Numerous funeral processions nudge shoppers and high-spirited children playing in the road.

Just below the grey walls of the temple is a long, low, whitewashed building that is Mother Teresa's Home for dying destitutes. A board at the entrance carries the name, Nirmal Hriday, the Place of the Pure Heart. There are no doors; it is always open. One enters directly into a reception area of sorts which is part of the men's ward, and is more often than not occupied by patients. The first impression, as one's eyes grow accustomed to the gloom, is of tiers of closely packed litters, a colourless, slow moving of people and a nameless smell that anti-septic cannot overpower. Then, individuals take shape : gauntly emerging from the anonymity of the hopelessly ill, or moving silently about their work. A boy carrying a bed-pan and soiled bandages. A Sister hurrying to a bedside. Two young men crouched over a prostrate form tenderly dressing a wound. Daylight shafts through the barred windows like rays of hope that fade and grow bright and dim and disappear.

A board hanging from a pillar has chalked on it the number of inmates, men and women. Through a door-way, past a nun with her sleeves rolled up, and some helpers toiling around vast vessels of food, is the women's ward, larger than the men's and suffused with the same quiet. There is no horror. The mind, shocked for a moment, easily accepts this new dimension. Here are people no longer tormented by fear, loneliness, degrada-tion, abandonment, but people cared for, loved and at peace. On the streets they would be objects of pity or revulsion, but under the sheltering roof of Nirmal Hriday, which is more truly the sheltering umbrella of the Missionaries of Charity, are old people, scarred people, critically ill people, but people. Without conscious effort, without a second thought, you can suddenly find yourself helping to do things you would never imagine you could 'do. Or would dare do under ordinary circumstances.

My many visits to Nirmal Hriday have been kaleidoscoped into a powerful image of incandescent serenity, a peace that really does pass understanding and of a beauty as mysterious as death itself. Mother Teresa tells of how the dying destitute, without anything to give and with a past of horror that should, understandably, embitter him for all time, will smile and say thank you and then die.

Perhaps the beauty, the strange radiance that one encounters in Nirmal Hriday is a coming to terms with death. A completely natural acceptance of the inevitable. Mother Teresa calls it going home. 'Nirmal Hriday,' she says, 'is really the treasure house of Calcutta. These people go to God straight away and when they go they tell Him about us. We help them to die with God. We help them to say sorry to God. To make peace with God according to their faith.' My own wavering faith has never allowed me to accept death as a going home or an adventure into some other life, possibly in some other form. I have met, particularly on the northern borders of India, people who are recognized and accepted as reincarnates, people who speak intelligently about their previous lives. The *Bardo* of Mahayana, the Paradise of Christianity, and the *Swarg* of Hinduism hold out for me neither the terror nor the promise of life everlasting. To me, death is the closing of a book, the fading of a flower. But in Nirmal Hriday, I can feel something : something, perhaps, as negative as an absence of fear, which could be the stirring of a belief itself.

There was the morning when we set out for Nirmal Hriday via the Mother House. I had woken depressed and in one of those frustrated bad tempers that come with the heat and the humidity of the monsoon. Mother was away somewhere and I was tempted to call it a day and go home. My photographer friend, Kalyan, persisted, and as we neared Kalighat I was driven to one of those excesses of self-pity that has one bordering on hysteria. It was no good. If I saw another dying destitute, another slum, experienced another bout of nose-rubbing ghastliness, I would revolt and abandon the entire project of the book. Suddenly there were the grey walls and silver roofs of Kalighat temple looming above us and, as we parked the car, a siege of beggars and near-naked children. I wanted to explode with anger. To get the hell out of there and go home to a bath and clean clothes. To the security of my familiar, upper-class surroundings.

Then there was the enveloping smell of the subterranean gloom of the Home for dying destitutes and a quite inexplicable falling away of all pressures. Someone, something, was draining me of all poison. I felt relaxed, secure. We were immediately drawn into the women's ward, though it is more usual to visit the men's ward first, since that is where one enters. A Sister was bending over an old woman who was refusing to eat or drink. Looking despairingly at us she said, 'She won't eat.' So I tried, noticing as I knelt beside the pathetic figure that there was no flesh, just skin papered to the bones. She kept her lips tightly clamped and the reason was in her eyes – an unblinking defiance prompted by some deep, insoluble hurt. There was nothing I could do to soften the pain. The Sisters, busy with other imperative calls upon their time and strength, returned and tried again. We all tried. But there was no response. I have often wondered since what became of her because, im-

mediately afterwards, I was distracted by a quite unexpected voice that said in a very crisp British accent,
'I say, do you have a fag?'

I looked around at the patients, most of them lying
spent and beyond talking, or crouched silently staring
at nothing in particular. Nearest me was an old woman
brown and crumpled like a raisin, with cropped white
hair and eyes rimmed with age who sat holding her
bleached nightdress about her as if she had been taken
unawares by a man in her boudoir. 'I beg your pardon?'
I found myself saying inanely, and once again there was
that very English voice asking if I had a fag. I have
never smoked in my life, but there I was, searching my
pockets in a hopeless endeavour to be helpful. My
companions, who smoke like chimneys, were out of
cigarettes, but hastened to get some. All the while she
sat there with a composure that would have done a
grande dame justice.

'You know,' she said very earnestly, 'they don't give
one fags here, but I do like the occasional one.' Amazed
as I was, I tried to look my casual best and began by
introducing myself formally. 'And I am Miss Murray,'
she said. 'I am a nurse. I was trained in Edinburgh,
that's Scotland, you know.' While I found myself groping
for something to say, she leaned forward as if to impart
a confidence and said, 'It's all right here, my dear, but,
frankly, I don't like the food. Too much oil. I'm not
complaining, of course, they are wonderful people.
They're doing extraordinary things. And that woman's
a saint, a saint, I tell you. But I would like some good
grub and a fag now and then. One does get a bit tired,
you know.'

A packet of cigarettes arrived and was handed over.
Miss Murray received it with almost ritualistic gracious-

ness, and then, crossing her legs and lighting a cigarette with studied care, took a first exaggerated puff. We had seen it before : Marlene Dietrich in *The Blue Angel,* we decided later. 'Aahh !' she said, 'that's good.'

I wondered what string of tragedies had brought the likes of Miss Murray into a home for dying destitutes. She might have heard me thinking because she said, 'I was living in this small room down there,' and she pointed way through the walls and her memories, 'when I had this stupid collapse.' A long pause then, 'Are you a doctor?' she asked suddenly. When I replied in the negative she said, 'Well, come closer. Look at me. Do you notice anything? I'm blind, you know, quite blind. I can see shadows, shapes, that's all. But that doesn't do, does it?' She puffed reflectively and added, 'It's good to be here with other people. It can be lonely, you know. And when the time comes, one needs people.' I asked her if there was anything we might do for her and she said, 'No, this is good enough,' holding up the packet of cigarettes and then, once again, as if to reassure us of her well-being she said, 'That Mother Teresa is a saint. She does such wonderful work.' It was difficult to leave her but we promised to return, knowing full well that when we did Miss Murray would have gone home.

My first memory of Nirmal Hriday is of Mother Teresa, with whom I went, personally admitting a man who lay dying on the steps outside. He had hardly been taken in when a Sister came and called Mother away. I followed, and there was the man from outside. Stripped of his rags he was one appalling wound alive with maggots. Mother sank down beside him and, with quiet efficiency, began to clean him as she talked to him caressingly in Bengali. A young man, very slight and with the beginnings of a beard, joined Mother and, without a word being said, handed her forceps, swabs and whatever she seemed to need from a kidney-bowl. I shall never forget the look on the man's face : pain changing to amazement and unashamed love. A Sister came hurriedly to Mother, whispered; Mother handed over to the young man and left, one gathered, in answer to a more urgent call. I remember I was surprised to find myself helping the young man and, eventually, when the dressing was done, I asked him who he was. There were no Brothers then. In a voice so gentle I hardly heard it, he said that he was a co-worker of Mother Teresa and that his name was Christo Das. Then he told me what I was to discover later is one of the most powerful motivating forces of the Missionaries of Charity : 'When I cleanse the wounds of the poor, I am cleansing the wounds of Christ.'

There was a service held in Nirmal Hriday that morning at which Christo Das and a few helpers like him received the Sacrament from a Jesuit priest. It was an extraordinary act of worship seen from where I knelt beside a dying man : the priest in white, a few patients propped up in prayer, framed by the tiers of litters and lit by a shaft of sunlight. Mother Teresa and her Sisters were far too occupied to join the service. They did not even genuflect when they passed the impromptu altar.

Once I accompanied Raghu Rai to take photographs at Nirmal Hriday. I went squirming with embarrassment since one is always conscious of being healthy and well fed in the company of these unfortunate people. To photograph them seemed an impossible outrage. But something incredible happened. The atmosphere of quiet understanding that prevails in Nirmal Hriday accepts even the probing eye of the camera. A woman sat sobbing soundlessly on her bed and Raghu Rai advanced slowly towards her, taking photographs as he went. I was beginning to think him distinctly callous, when he dropped his camera and took hold of the gnarled hands held out towards him. 'Why do you cry, Mother?' he asked, sitting beside her. Immediately she stopped crying and looking intently at him asked, 'Is it you, my son?'

'Yes, Mother, it is I.'

'You've been a long time. I thought you would never come.'

'Now I am here. Don't worry any more.'

'Are you married?'

'Yes, and I have children. I tell them about you.'

The old lady smiled toothlessly and reaching her hands towards Raghu's neck touched his forehead to hers. 'God bless you, my son,' she said, 'Now I can die happy.'

In the car returning from Nirmal Hriday, Raghu impetuously told Mother Teresa, 'I did not believe much in God and things. But today, Mother, I do.' The quiet smile she gave in answer was a thankful prayer. I could almost hear her saying, 'They have so little but they give so much.'

I had occasion to take a visiting English Lord to Nirmal Hriday. He had asked to see the 'real' Calcutta and expressed a wish to be shown what positive steps were being taken to combat poverty and suffering. It was winter and he was wearing a three-piece suit. We had hardly entered the building when a Sister unceremoniously asked us to move back because the dead were being brought out. Even as what she said sank into our astonished minds, a file of people carrying pathetically small bundles of white cloth brushed past. My guest was visibly shocked. He was silent for most of the time while we were in Nirmal Hriday but, as we were about to enter the magnificent limousine provided by the local British High Commission, he told me with genuine sincerity that he wished he was less well clad and fed. 'This suit burns me,' he said.

The extraordinary spirit of Nirmal Hriday now reaches out to wherever the Missionaries of Charity work. One morning, we accompanied two Sisters to their small dispensary and feeding centre near the busy Sealdah Station. Sealdah has resisted several shock waves of refugees coming from what was East Pakistan, now Bangladesh. But the refugees have invariably won by occupying every lane and sidewalk and open space in the vicinity. For months on end in the past they have lived on the platforms of the busy station while official-dom fought desperately to find ways and means to re-habilitate them. It has been an almost unending battle since 1947, and one that the world has failed to recog-nize but has often criticized.

Imagine Charing Cross or Grand Central or the Gare du Nord beset every day by thousands upon thousands of starving, homeless refugees. Occupying kiosks, benches, lounges, restaurants, and raising hovels on the platforms, cooking, bathing and defecating there. Relief organiza-tions fling themselves into action distributing food and clothing, providing limited shelter for a lucky few. Newspapers scream in headlines and editorials. TV watches with baleful eyes. But they keep coming, spill-ing out of the station to settle where they can. The relief organizations call up reserves. Urgent appeals go out. The law is dismayed into taking no action because what action can it take? Charge every unfortunate man, woman and child with vagrancy? Unlawful occupation of land? Loitering? So the gaols are filled, the hospitals are filled, the homes for the poor are filled. And they keep coming, hungry and homeless. What then? Friends near and far send clothes, blankets, food and toys – yes, toys. They keep coming. They have nothing. Nothing to lose. And a city's resources are inadequate. A country's means too small. A world's conscience too fazed or its will too politically influenced.

In her own small way Mother Teresa has tried to help by sending her Sisters to feed the starving and administer to the sick at Sealdah. As Father Henry would say, 'Theirs has been an infiltration of love.'

Opposite the dispensary, something of a small settlement has grown up where the very poor wait to be fed and treated. Some of them have even been pressed into collecting green coconut shells for Prem Daan, so there is a great pile of shells near by on which very small children play.

We watched a queue forming for medicines and then accompanied one of the Sisters to the near-by station where she felt there must be one or two people in need of urgent help. We found a man crouching just outside the entrance, so spent he could not even speak when the Sister talked to him. So she summoned a passing rickshaw, but when the rickshaw puller saw his intended fare he began protesting that he could not possibly pick up someone so filthy and so ill. The Sister and a growing crowd prevailed; someone came forward to lift the man into the rickshaw and they were soon lost in a sea of people. I walked into the station and strolled half the length of a shadowy platform before returning to the dispensary. A Sister was pulling a white sheet over a prone figure in the queue of patients as I approached, and I knew instinctively that it was the man who had been rescued just minutes before.

'He's got his ticket; we never say people die,' said a

. . . then clasped her by both shoulders speaking gently to
her all the while

In the twenty-seven years since she left the shelter of Loreto
Convent, Mother Teresa has received several awards

To Mother Teresa, whose life is a living prayer, the need to
withdraw, to be alone with God, is as important as her work

Sister joyfully. 'I'm sure he went straight to heaven. It was lucky we found him. He died so peacefully. We just made him comfortable, gave him some water and he smiled and was gone. I'm sure he got his ticket straight to heaven.'

The shock I should have felt at finding someone dead in a queue of living did not register. There was no fuss, no remorse, no fear. People sitting next to the corpse hardly noticed. The work of examination and dispensing medicine went on. Had the man lived a little longer he would have been sent to Nirmal Hriday. Had he not been found by the good Sisters he would have died unloved and unattended on a city street.

It is difficult to believe now, when moving about with the Missionaries of Charity, that they were once resented and faced considerable opposition. Sister Bernard, with whom we visited the leper colony at Titagarh, remembers how 'People would even threaten to kill Mother, but she would just walk through the crowds. She was never frightened. Then, when it was seen that so much good was being done to all people, regardless of caste or creed, they began to accept us. Soon people who had been against us in Kalighat were coming to Nirmal Hriday with small gifts of food. It was usually on festival days when they were going to offer *puja* at the Kali temple. It was an outlet for their charity and it brought happiness and consolation to our people.'

There was a time when it was thought that Mother Teresa and her Missionaries were converting the dying to Christianity. But it needs only a glance at the records that are kept to see that Christians are in the minority at Nirmal Hriday. I remember being present once as an old man died in the Home for dying destitutes. He was a Hindu. I can still see a Brother crouched over

M.T. – E

him, wetting his lips with water from the sacred Ganges.
I have asked Mother about this and she has made it
abundantly clear that those who die in her Homes are
given whatever comfort they ask and it is possible to
give according to their beliefs. Sister Bernard told us
how arrangements are made for Muslim burials and
Hindu cremations through religious agencies. This, of
course, does not prevent the good Missionaries from
adding their own dimension of love and devotion. Sister
Bernard recalls how quite recently Sister Luke, who is
very devoted, received lots of flowers on her Feast Day,
and yet she had none. So we asked her what had happened to the flowers and she said that there had been
about twelve deaths in Nirmal Hriday during the day
and no one had come to remove the bodies. So, she
garlanded them with her flowers because she was sad
that there was no one to mourn them because no one
had tears for them.

Father Henry remembers how a young Anglo-Indian
girl used to press him for a job. According to him, 'She
looked a shy, miserable creature.' Quite hopeless for any
work he had to give. Then, one day, Mother Teresa
asked him to send her a Bengali woman to help in
Nirmal Hriday. 'The Anglo-Indian girl comes to me
and I have a wicked thought,' said Father Henry. 'I'll
send her to Nirmal Hriday and in two days' time she'll
run away and I'll get rid of her.' So he sent her and a
few days later he had a report that there had seldom been
anyone who had worked so hard and so devotedly. She
remained not for the expected two days but for six
months and then asked Mother Teresa if she might join
the Order. And she was gladly accepted. 'For those who
love God,' added Father Henry, 'everything finally takes
a good turn. Even your weak side. Even your stupidity.'

Another person who came and stayed at Nirmal Hriday was a young boy, abandoned and very sick, whom some Brothers picked up at Howrah Station and sent to the Home for dying destitutes. Miraculously, he recovered but refused to leave. Instead he remained to help care for those he had learned to love, living and eating with the patients and finding time to go first to school, and later to college.

Just inside the entrance to Nirmal Hriday, is a small illuminated glass case in which reposes a statue of the Virgin Mary, quite unlike any other in that it wears the ribbon and medal of the Padmashree, the Indian Order of the Lotus. Mother Teresa was given the award in 1962, the first non-Indian ever to receive it. She became an Indian citizen in 1948.

In the twenty-seven years since she left the shelter of Loreto Convent, Mother Teresa has received several awards : the Nehru Award (1969), the Magsaysay Award (1962), the Pope John XXIII Peace Prize (1971) and the Templeton Award (1973), in recognition of her crusade among the world's deprived. A very different kind of award was a limousine presented to Mother Teresa by Pope Paul VI at the conclusion of the Eucharistic Congress in Bombay in 1964. It was no ordinary limousine and no ordinary presentation. The car, a 1964 Ford Lincoln, had been especially designed and manufactured, just one of its kind, and was a gift to the Pope from the American people. When, after using it for a brief few hours he presented it to Mother Teresa, he did so, in his own words, 'To share in her universal mission of love'.

No one knowing Mother Teresa could imagine her or her Missionaries driving around in a sleek, cruiser-sized, white car. It was clearly meant as a gift to raise funds for her rapidly expanding mission. An outright sale would have raised a useful lakh of rupees (£7500). Mother Teresa had a better idea. She sought, and received, permission from the Government to raffle the car, and that in a unique way : every donation of one hundred rupees (about £13) or more, to her Mission, was acknowledged with a numbered receipt. The target was four thousand such donations, but in the time it took to close the raffle, it was over-subscribed. And so the Pope's limousine, aptly named the 'People's Car', raised almost five lakhs of rupees (£37,500) and was won by a young Indian chartered accountant studying at the time in Britain.

A charming recollection attaches to this raffle. Several people who made donations promised Mother Teresa that if they won the car they would return it to her to re-raffle. Among them was the then Governor of West Bengal. Mother admitted to having prayed that one of these generous souls would be the lucky winner but then, in her extraordinary matter-of-fact way she said cheerfully that the Lord must have wished otherwise. As it was she had raised the money she required to start one of her most cherished ventures – Shantinagar, the Home for lepers.

It was while returning from Shantinagar with Mother Teresa in her old pick-up van that she disarmingly talked about the possibility of her being awarded the Nobel Peace Prize : the news of her name being included in the final short list of nominees had been making the front page in all Indian newspapers. If she did get it, the money would be spent in founding new Homes for dying destitutes, abandoned children, alcoholics, drug addicts, lepers, and generally for her people, the poorest of the poor, in whichever part of the world they might be. She told me that Mrs Ghandi had very generously allowed her, in the past, to keep some of the money she received by way of foreign awards abroad, so it could be used for her Missions outside India.

'You know,' she continued, as disarmingly, 'these awards are not for me, they are for my people. That is why they don't affect me at all. Because I know they are not for me. It is for the poor people who are being recognized. They are becoming wanted. Loved. The whole world is beginning to know about it. The very fact that so much is being written means the people are getting involved.'

9. A Vocabulary of Love

The book began with a prayer. It was Mother Teresa's idea. If there was to be a book about her work, it was obviously God's wish and should have His blessing. So it was arranged that we attend an evening service of Adoration in the Mother House. We had hardly arrived and were awaiting Mother in the parlour, when the electricity failed – a not unusual occurrence in Calcutta where regular load-shedding is resorted to in an attempt to conserve power. Mother conducted us to the chapel, leading us up the stairs by candlelight. Candles lit the chapel, flickering on the austere altar, on the small organ and on the floor where we knelt. The gentle orange glow, run through every now and then by the harsh sweep of headlights from the street outside, lent a remarkable serenity to a beautiful service.

Mother had selected my favourite prayer and my favourite hymn, a rousing, happy, infectious song, and there was a special prayer for the four of us who would be writing, recording and photographing in the course of the book. 'We offer You all the thoughts of our minds, the affections of our hearts . . . Let us hear Your voice and attend to Your holy inspiration.' If one could only have started writing then and there, among that innocence of shadowy nuns raising their voices to the glory of God and in the presence of the founder of this incredible far-reaching Order.

If we could only have captured the aura of those candlelit faces, the intensity of Mother's devotion and the suffusing sense of peace . . . Our cameras tried and failed, and our words, removed from that service, lost much of the magic and the immediate inspiration.

Mother Teresa and Sister Agnes knelt side by side, the founder and her first postulant, embraced by the light of a single candle. As I watched their faces enriched by prayer, I understood how much these soothing moments with God mean to people who have devoted their lives to the unending demands and tragedies of the poorest of the poor. Sister Agnes had said, 'Every day we have Mass, half an hour of meditation, morning prayer, afternoon prayer, and in the evening we have a full hour of Adoration. It would not be possible to work otherwise. There must be a spiritual motive. You can work only for God. You can never work for any man.'

To Mother Teresa, whose life is a living prayer, the need to withdraw, to be alone with God, is as important as her work. 'That is why we begin and end the day with prayer, because, when we pray, we are touching the body of Christ. You people in the world might not have the time or the leisure to pray. It is a beautiful gift of God for us to have that amount of time.' How typical of Mother Teresa to see her all-consuming work as allowing time for prayer, where the likes of us might be far too busy, too preoccupied to find time to communicate with our Maker.

Prayer was the subject of one of our many discussions. I must feel eternally grateful for all the time that Mother Teresa has allowed me just as I must feel for ever guilty at having taken up so much of it. No one I know who has ever met Mother Teresa, for however short a while, has been unmoved by the experience. For some, it has meant a completely new way of life; for me, it has been one of the most extraordinary experiences of a fairly eventful life. She has taught me to see, not merely to look, to appreciate, not merely to understand and she has consolidated whatever faith I had. I can think of no one I would like to have with me more when I am in real need or when my time is up than Mother Teresa because, for me, she has, I suppose unconsciously, built up a powerful vocabulary of understanding, which even as a non-practising Christian I can comfortingly use.

ON CONVERSION

'Oh, I hope I am converting. I don't mean what you think. I hope we are converting hearts. Not even Almighty God can convert a person unless that person wants it. What we are all trying to do by our work, by serving the people, is to come closer to God. If in coming face to face with God we accept Him in our lives, then we are converting. We become a better Hindu, a better Muslim, a better Catholic, a better whatever we are, and then by being better we come closer and closer to Him. If we accept Him fully in our lives, then that is conversion. What approach would I use? For me, naturally, it would be a Catholic one, for you it may be Hindu, for someone else, Buddhist, according to one's conscience. What God is in your mind you must accept. But I cannot prevent myself from trying to give you what I have.

'I am not afraid to say I am in love with Jesus because He is everything to me. But you may have a different picture in your life. And this is the way that conversion has to be understood – people think that conversion is just changing overnight. It is not like that. Nobody, not even your father or your mother, can make you do that. Not even Almighty God can force a person. Even Jesus, though He was God Himself, could not convert the hearts of the people unless they allowed Him to.

'I want very much people to come to know God, to love Him, to serve Him, for that is true happiness. And what I have I want everyone in the world to have. But it is their choice. If they have seen the light they can follow it. I cannot give them the light : I can only give the means. If I breathe into Kalighat and do some work there and really serve the people with great love and sacrifice, then naturally they will begin to think of God. Once they think, they will come to know, and knowing, they will want to love, and if they love they will want to serve.

'There are many Hindu ladies who want our way of life, the life of poverty, prayer, sacrifice and service. They want the life of a Missionary. But they wish to retain their faith, their own belief in God. Now I don't know how this works – you see, they want to take vows, they want prayer, they want complete dedication. I am trying to think of a way.

'We are not social workers, though we do social work.'

ON BELIEF

'What we allow God to use us for, that is important. What He is doing through us, that is important. Because we are religious and our vocation is not to work for the lepers or the dying, our vocation is to belong to

Jesus. Because I belong to Him, the work is a means for me to put my love for Him into action. So it is not an end, it is a means. Because my vocation is to belong to God properly, love Him with undivided love and chastity, I take the vows.

'I see Christ in every person I touch because He has said, "I was hungry, I was thirsty, I was naked, I was sick, I was suffering, I was homeless and you took me . . ." It is as simple as that. Every time I give a piece of bread, I give it to Him. That is why we must find a hungry one, and a naked one. That is why we are totally bound to the poor.

'The vows we take make our religious life. Our vow of chastity is nothing but our undivided love for Christ in chastity, then we proceed to the freedom of poverty – poverty is nothing but freedom. And that total surrender is obedience. If I belong to God, if I belong to Christ, then He must be able to use me. That is obedience. Then we give whole-hearted service to the poor. That is service. They complete each other. That is our life.

'If you really belong to the work that has been entrusted to you, then you must do it with your whole heart. And you can bring salvation only by being honest and by really working with God. It is not how much we are doing but how much love, how much honesty, how much faith, is put into doing it. It makes no difference what we are doing. What you are doing, I cannot do, and what I am doing, you cannot do. But all of us are doing what God has given us to do. Only sometimes we forget and we spend more time looking at somebody else and wishing we were doing something else.

'We waste our time thinking of tomorrow and today we let the day pass and yesterday is gone.'

ON LOVE

'The poor must know that we love them, that they are wanted. They themselves have nothing to give but love. We are concerned with how to get this message of love and compassion across. We are trying to bring peace to the world through our work. But the work is the gift of God, eh?

'People today are hungry for love, for understanding love which is much greater and which is the only answer to loneliness and great poverty. That is why we are able to go to countries like England and America and Australia where there is no hunger for bread. But there, people are suffering from terrible loneliness, terrible despair, terrible hatred, feeling unwanted, feeling helpless, feeling hopeless. They have forgotten how to smile, they have forgotten the beauty of the human touch. They are forgetting what is human love. They need someone who will understand and respect them.

'The poor are not respected. People do not think that the poor can be treated as people who are lovable, as people like you and I.

'You know, the young are beginning to understand. They want to serve with their hands, and to love with their hearts. To the full, not superficially.

'Love can be misused for selfish motives. I love you, but at the same time I want to take from you as much as I can, even the things that are not for me to take. Then there is no true love any more. True love hurts. It always has to hurt. It must be painful to love someone, painful to leave them, you might have to die for them. When people marry they have to give up everything to love each other. The mother who gives birth to her child suffers much. It is the same for us in religious life. To belong fully to God we have to give up everything. Only then can we truly love. The word "love" is so misunderstood and so misused.

'A young American couple told me once, "You know a lot about love; you must be married." And I said, "Yes, but sometimes I find it difficult to smile at Him."'

ON DEATH

'Death is going home, yet people are afraid of what will come so they do not want to die. If we do, if there is no mystery, we will not be afraid. There is also the question of conscience – "I could have done better." Very often as we live, so we die. Death is nothing but a continuation of life, the completion of life. The surrendering of the human body. But the heart and the soul live for ever. They do not die. Every religion has got eternity – another life; this life is not the end; people who believe it is, fear death. If it was properly explained that death was nothing but going home to God, then there would be no fear.'

ON NIRMAL HRIDAY

'We help the poor die with God. We help them to say sorry to God. It is between them and God alone. Nobody else. Nobody has the right to come in at that time. We just help them to make their peace with God because that is the greatest need – to die in peace with God. We live that they may die, so that they may go home according to what is written in the book, be it written according to Hindu, or Muslim, or Buddhist, or Catholic, or Protestant, or any other belief. There are societies who collect their own dead; we have never had any trouble.

'Nobody in Nirmal Hriday has died depressed, in despair, unwanted, unfed or unloved. That is why I think this is the treasure-house of Calcutta. We give them whatever they ask according to their faith. Some ask for Ganges water, some for Holy Water, for a word or for a prayer. We try and give them whatever they want. Some just ask for an apple, or bread, or a cigarette. Others just want somebody to sit with them.

'In the beginning we weren't accepted at all, we had quite a lot of trouble. At one time some young people were going around threatening and destroying and our people were getting more and more frightened. One day I said, "If this is the way you want it, kill me, I will go straight to heaven. But you must stop this nonsense. You cannot go on like this." After that, it finished. It was all right.

'We had one of the priests from the temple who died here very beautifully. The others could not understand because he was so bitter when he came in, very bitter and he was so young, only twenty-four or twenty-five. He was the head priest, I think. No hospital would take him in. He was thrown out. This is why he was so bitter. He did not want to die when he came, but he changed. He became quiet and peaceful. He was with us only two weeks and people from the temple used to come and visit him every day. They could not believe the change in him. I suppose, surrounded by people who were suffering in the same way, he learned to accept. The people themselves are of tremendous help to each other.

I often wonder that if innocent people did not suffer so much what would happen to the world? They are the ones who are interceding the whole time. Their innocence is so pleasing to God. By accepting suffering, they intercede for us.'

ON FAITH

'Why these people and not me? That person picked up from the drain, why is he here, why not me? That is the mystery. Nobody can give that answer. But it is not for us to decide; only God can decide life and death. The healthy person may be closer to dying or even more dead than the person who is dying. They might be spiritually dead, only it doesn't show. Who are we to decide?

'That is why abortion is such a terrible sin. You are not only killing life, but putting self before God; yet people decide who has to live and who has to die. They want to make themselves almighty God. They want to take the power of God in their hands. They want to say, "I can do without God. I can decide." That is the most devilish thing that a human hand can do. That is why we are paying with such terrible things happening in the world. It is a punishment, it is the cry of those children continually coming before God. It is such a contradiction of even ordinary common sense and reason : we spend millions to prolong the life of an old person who is more or less dead. And yet there is this young life for the future . . . I cannot understand. There is no way to express it. We are fighting abortion by adoption. In the same way, I cannot understand capital punishment.

'Where there is mystery, there must be faith. Faith, you cannot change no matter how you look at it. Either you have it, or you don't. For us, it is very simple because our feet are on the ground. We have more of the living reality. There was a time when the Church had to show majesty and greatness. But today, people have found that it does not pay. They have found the emptiness of all that pomp so they are coming down more to the ground, and in coming down there is the danger that they are not finding their proper place.

'God has created all things. All the butterflies, the animals – the whole of nature He has created for us. To them He has not given the will power to choose. They have only an instinct. Animals can be very lovable and love very beautifully, but that is out of instinct. But the human being can choose. That is the one thing that God does not take from us. The will power, the power to will. I want to go to heaven and I will, with the grace of God. If I choose to commit sin and go to hell, that is my choice. God cannot force me to do otherwise. That's why when we become religious we give up that will power. That is why the sacrifice is so great : the vow of obedience is very difficult. Because in making that vow you surrender the only thing that is your own – your will power. Otherwise my health, my body, my eyes, my everything are all His and He can take them. I can fall, I can break, but my will power doesn't go like this. I must choose to give it and that is beautiful.

'Our expanding knowledge does not dim our faith, it only shows the size of God's creation. Often we cannot understand. I don't know if you have read St Augustine's life : it is a beautiful example. St Augustine was struggling to understand God, to understand the

Trinity, to understand the magnitude of God's creation. His human mind could not grasp it. He was searching here and there when he came upon a small boy, who was trying to fill water into a hole in the ground. St Augustine asked him what he was doing and the boy said, "I'm trying to fill this hole with water." And St Augustine said it was impossible. Then the child, who, in truth, was an angel, said, "It is still easier to put the ocean into this hole than for you to understand the mystery of God." And it is true.'

ON HER WORK

'Since we began our work, something wonderful is happening. More and more poor people are coming from the villages into Calcutta, but there is a difference. Ordinary people are beginning to get concerned. Before, they used to pass by a person dying on the streets, but now, when they see something like that, they immediately do something. If they can't get an ambulance, they bring the person to us by rickshaw, or taxi, or take them to Kalighat, or they phone us. The big thing is that they do something; it's wonderful, eh? At least it has broadened people's minds. And they are no longer frightened. They used to be frightened before of getting involved with the police, but they know now that there is a place to go to and that there are Sisters who will stand by them.

'We do not only help the dying, but the living also. There's Shishu Bhavan, our dispensaries and our schools ...

'I did not know that our work would grow so fast or go so far. I never doubted that it would live, but I did not think it would be like this. Doubt I never had, because I had this conviction that if God blesses it, it will prosper. Humanly speaking, it is impossible, out of the question. Because none of us has got the experience. None of us has got the things that the world looks for. This is the miracle of all those little Sisters all around the world. God is using them – they are just little instruments in His hands. But they have their conviction. As long as any of us has this conviction we are all right. The work will prosper. But the moment we begin to say "It is I, it is my work", then it becomes selfish. Nothing will be necessary. The Congregation and the work will die.

'That is why we begin with this conviction; that is why we need the Eucharist, we need Jesus – to deepen our faith. If we can see Jesus in the appearance of bread, we can see Him in the broken bodies of the poor. That is why we need that oneness with Christ, why we need that deep faith in Christ. It is very beautiful. When we have that deepening of contact with Christ and can accept Him fully, we can touch the broken bodies. We put it into practice straight away. You need the poor to touch Him. You feed yourself in the Eucharist and after you are fed you want to use that energy, to give it out. That is why you see the Sisters run, they never walk. They call us a "running Congregation".'

ON SIN

'God dwells in us. That's what gives Him a beautiful power. It doesn't matter where you are as long as you are clean of heart. He is there with you and within you twenty-four hours. That's why He says, "Love others like I love you." Clean of heart means openness, that complete freedom, that detachment that allows you to love God without hindrance, without obstacles. When sin comes into our life that is a personal obstacle between me and God. He cannot act through me or give me strength when there is sin between us. Sin is nothing but slavery.

'When I choose evil, I sin. That's where my will comes in. When I seek something for myself at the cost of everything else, I deliberately choose sin. I say, for example, that I am tempted to tell a lie, and then I accept to tell the lie. Well, my mind is impure. I have burdened myself. I have put an obstacle between me and God. That lie has won. I preferred the lie to God. That's why poverty is such a wonderful gift of God for all of us – there are fewer obstacles. Very often, in a desire to get something, there's greed, there's jealousy, there's distraction. We cannot see God then. It is an obstacle.

'More than any other Congregation, we need poverty, real poverty. It gives us the detachment and the real freedom necessary to understand the very poor people with whom we work.'

ON PRAYER

'You should spend at least half an hour in the morning, and an hour at night in prayer. You can pray while you work. Work doesn't stop prayer, and prayer doesn't stop work. It requires only that small raising of mind to Him. "I love you, God, I trust you, I believe in you, I need you now." Small things like that. They are wonderful prayers.'

*

As we wrote this book, Dubby's father sickened and died. He was a well-known and well-loved person, a General in the Indian Army, with the distinction of having won India's first Victoria Cross in World War II. A young second-lieutenant at the time, Premindra Singh Bhagat was given the award 'For the longest feat of sheer, cold courage'.

As his father lay critically ill in a Calcutta hospital, Dubby, a Hindu remember, phoned me from his bed-side and asked if I would get in touch immediately with Sister Agnes : Mother Teresa was away at the time. 'Just tell her that I want her to know,' he said, 'and she'll know what to do.' I had no need for lengthy explanations. Almost as if she knew, Sister Agnes said, 'We'll pray for him. There is nothing else we can do. But tell your friend that all of us will remember his father in our prayers.' They were amazingly comforting words, not only to Dubby but to his entire family. Somehow, the knowledge that the Missionaries of Charity were praying for General Bhagat seemed to remove some of the anguish, some of the fear from the minds of all those who stood helplessly about him.

When General Bhagat died, Mother Teresa, who had returned to Calcutta, suggested that she hold a Mass for him. To Dubby who went to give her the news she said, 'You know, his work must have been finished. God wanted him so He took him home.'

The important thing about this is that Dubby, who had once told Mother how scared he was of death, faced up to his father's death and the harrowing days that followed with a calm quite alien to him. I believe that Mother Teresa and her Missionaries of Charity had, during the weeks we had spent with them, given Dubby a new dimension of understanding.

Mother Teresa chose the service of Resurrection for the Mass. A Jesuit priest spoke of courage, a quality that was needed more than ever in the warring, confused world of today. He remembered the example of General Bhagat who had lived courageously. It was a beautifully simple little service with comforting prayers and responses and hymns full of encouragement and hope. Mrs Bhagat, her mother, Dubby and his sister and a support of relatives and friends were deeply moved.

There had been other services, other rituals, all heavy with a sense of grief and loss. This simple Mass in the Mother House of the Missionaries of Charity was as sincere as a blessing and as triumphant as the spirit of the service – the Resurrection.

After the service that morning, Mother gave Dubby a prayer book of the Missionaries of Charity. She had inscribed it in her powerful hand :

God loves you with a special love.
Love others as He loves you.

God bless you.
Mother Teresa MC

Epilogue

The last time I met Mother Teresa she was quite seriously ill. She came down to the parlour to meet me looking distinctly spent and more tired than I can ever remember having seen her. Yet, throughout our meeting she made no mention of her ailment – I learned later that she had a temperature of a hundred and five degrees when she agreed to see me. Her Sisters were very anxious and, without actually saying it, implied how stubborn Mother is in times like this. They would have liked a doctor, but Mother had instructed them not to send for one.

There seemed only one thing to do : call a doctor. But would Mother see him? And even if she did, would she take his medicines? I had been told before how Mother tears up prescriptions the minute they have been written, or hides them. I can only suggest that so strong is her belief that she leaves herself entirely in the hands of God. But then, I remember Father Henry saying, 'She's a stubborn woman.'

The doctor we appealed to has known Mother Teresa for years. Before he met her, he was sceptical of her work, implying that she and her Missionaries of Charity might be doing more harm than good – medically speaking. Then he met her and saw her work and, though he'd hate the description, being as stubborn and practical as Mother herself, became a devotee. It was he who, some years ago, more or less abducted Mother from the Mother House where she lay on the verge of collapse, and locked her up in a nursing home. So he knew how to deal with Mother. In the company of a happily startled Sister, he strode into Mother's room, examined her and said by way of explanation that he'd had a prayer whispered in his ear. Some equally determined nuns made sure that the prescription had no time to disappear.

The point of this story is that between Mother Teresa and Calcutta and, more recently, the world, there is a two-way traffic of understanding and help. Her most desperate moments, her Gethsemanes, were mainly during the earliest days of her Mission, when she was entirely alone but for her faith, and when she wrote in her diary, 'Friday. Talked to X who had said he had come to school on an empty stomach. They have nothing to eat at home. I gave him the money for my tram fare to buy some food, and walked home in the evening.' Or again, 'Today I learned a good lesson. The poverty of the poor must be so hard for them. While looking for a home (for a centre) I walked and walked till my arms and legs ached. I thought how much they must ache in body and soul looking for a home, food and health. Then the comfort of Loreto came to tempt me. But of free choice, my God, and out of love for You, I desire to remain and do whatever be Your holy will in my regard. Give me courage now, this moment.' One wonders how many other Missionaries had walked out like her, all alone, into the vastness of India or the terrifying uncertainty of a great city. Chance, or Providence, or God Himself, view it as you will, failed them and they went unnoticed, however brave their endeavour. It could be that Mother Teresa's belief was stronger than theirs or that, as she herself explains, she had the certainty of God's call and knew that He would not fail her. That same Chance, or Providence, or God, brought people to help her, from the well-known and famous, to the unknown and anonymous; students, diplomatic wives, Government officials, ministers and businessmen. So, Bengal's most powerful Chief Minister could tell a journalist on his eightieth birthday, 'As I climbed the stairs leading to my office, I was thinking of Mother Teresa who devotes her entire life to the service of the poor.' The Railway Minister himself presented Mother Teresa with passes that allow her and her Sisters to travel free on the Indian Railways. We know that Calcutta's Police Commissioner championed her cause at a time when there was a great deal of opposition to her work. A senior Bengal Government official saw Mother Teresa over some insurmountable hurdles throughout those difficult early years when even a person of her indomitable courage could have been defeated by an inflexible person armed with the letter of the law.

Jawaharlal Nehru, who inaugurated Mother Teresa's children's Home in New Delhi, when asked by Mother if she could tell him about her work said, 'No, Mother, you need not. I know about it. That's why I'm here.'

What must always amaze one is that while a growing number of people reached out their hands to help Mother Teresa, she alone was touching and helping them, and through them was reaching out to the vast multitude of the poorest poor.

Now she has become something of a household name in Calcutta, if not in the rest of India and the world. Indeed, she is being written and talked about in India as The Mother, which sets her instantly among the living saints. Not far from the Mother House on Lower Circular Road, is a shrine under a tree where Mother Teresa's portrait reposes with images and prints of Jesus and the Virgin Mary. The good nuns are all very embarrassed by this. And yet, I remember, many years ago when it had all hardly begun, I was seated next to a Calcutta socialite who was discussing her latest charity. I asked her if she had heard of Mother Teresa. She paused, looked quizzically surprised, and said, 'Yes, I have, actually. She's something of a saint, isn't she?'

Chronological Table

Days in the Lives of the Missionaries of Charity

27 August 1910 Born Agnes Gonxha Bejaxhiu, of
Albanian parents at Skopje, Yugoslavia. There were
three children, one boy and two girls. She attended
the Government (Gimnaziya) school. While at school,
she became a member of the Sodality. At that time,
Yugoslav Jesuits had accepted to work in the Calcutta
Archdiocese. The first group arrived in Calcutta on
30 December 1925. One of them was sent to Kur-
seong. From there he sent enthusiastic letters about
the Bengal Mission field. Those letters were read
regularly to the Sodalists. Young Agnes was one of
the Sodalists who volunteered for the Bengal Mission.
She was put in touch with the Loreto nuns in Ireland
as they were working in the Calcutta Archdiocese.

29 November 1928 She was sent to Loreto Abbey,
Rathfarnham, Dublin, Ireland, and from there was
sent to India to begin her novitiate in Darjeeling.

6 January 1929–18 August 1948 She taught geography
at St Mary's High School in Calcutta. For some years
she was Principal of the School. She was also in
charge of the Daughters of St Anne, the Indian religious order attached to the Loreto Sisters.

24 May 1931 She took her first vows in Darjeeling.

24 May 1937 She took her final vows in Loreto School,
Darjeeling.

10 September 1946 'Inspiration Day' when, on a train

to Darjeeling, Mother heard the call of God.

January 1948   Mother Teresa requested permission from her Superior to live outside the cloister and work in the Calcutta slums. She applied to Rome in February 1948.

18 August 1948   Mother Teresa laid aside her Loreto habit and clothed herself in a white sari with a blue border and a cross on the shoulder. She went to Patna for three months to the American Medical Missionary Sisters for intensive nursing training. By Christmas she was back in Calcutta and living with the Little Sisters of the Poor.

21 December 1948   Mother Teresa opened her first slum school in Moti Jheel.

1948   Mother Teresa became an Indian citizen.

February 1949   She moved into a flat in a private house owned by the Gomes family.

19 March 1949   The first recruit, a young Bengali girl named Subhasini Das, arrived.

7 October 1950   The new Congregation of the Missionaries of Charity was approved and instituted in Calcutta, and from there spread throughout India. This was the date of the founding of the Mother House at 54A Lower Circular Road, Calcutta.

September 1962   Received the Padmashree Award from the President of India and also the Magsaysay Award for International Understanding given in honour of the late President of the Philippines.

25 March 1963   The Archbishop of Calcutta blessed the beginnings of a new branch, the Missionary Brothers of Charity.

December 1964   The Pope donated the car used by him at the Eucharistic Congress in Bombay to Mother

Teresa and her charities.

1 February 1965 The Missionaries of Charity became a Society of Pontifical Right.

26 July 1965 To Venezuela to open a centre near Caracas.

8 December 1967 To Ceylon to open a centre in Colombo.

22 August 1968 To Rome to open a centre in the slums of that city.

8 September 1968 To Tanzania to open a centre in Tabora.

26 March 1969 The International Association of Co-Workers of Mother Teresa was affiliated to the Order of the Missionaries of Charity and the Constitution of the Association was presented to His Holiness Pope Paul VI and received his blessing.

13 September 1969 To Bourke, Australia to open a centre for Aborigines.

26 April 1970 To Australia to begin work in Melbourne.

16 July 1970 To Jordan to begin work in Amman.

8 December 1970 A Novitiate was opened in England to train novices from Europe and the Americas.

6 January 1971 Awarded Pope John XXIII Peace Prize by Pope Paul VI.

14 July 1971 House opened in Paddington, London.

25 August 1971 Ceylon centre closed.

September 1971 Received the Good Samaritan Award in Boston, USA.

16 October 1971 Received the John F. Kennedy International Award.

28 October 1971 Awarded Doctor of Humane Letters Degree in Washington.

October 1971 Opened House in Belfast, Ulster, and the

Bronx, New York on 19 October.

21 January 1972   Centres opened in Bangladesh.

25 March 1972   Novitiate opened in Melbourne, Australia.

15 August 1972   Convent opened in Mauritius.

15 November 1972   Presented with Jawaharlal Nehru Award for 1969 for International Understanding by the Indian Government.

26 February 1973   Centre opened in Gaza, Israel.

27 February 1973   The Brothers opened a centre in South Viet Nam.

25 March 1973   Centre opened in Katherine, N.T., Australia.

25 April 1973   Templeton Award for 'Progress in Religion' presented by Prince Philip.

22 August 1973   Centre opened in Hodeida, Yemen.

August 1973   Novitiate for Europe and the Americas transferred to Rome.

18 September 1973   Belfast centre closed.

4 October 1973   Centre opened in Lima, Peru.

23 November 1973   Foundation in Addis Ababa, Ethiopia.

3 April 1974   The Brothers opened a centre in Phnom Penh, Cambodia.

9 June 1974   Centre opened in Palermo, Sicily.

19 June 1974   'Mater et Magistra' Award presented to Mother Teresa in America. Third Order of St Francis of Assisi.

18 July 1974   Centre opened in Papua, New Guinea.

1 January 1975   Novitiate for Brothers opened in Viet Nam.

May 1975   Brothers withdrawn from South Viet Nam and Cambodia.

June 1975 Brother Andrew leaves South Viet Nam and Cambodia.

19 June–2 July 1975 Mother Teresa attended World Conference of International Women's Year in Mexico as a member of the Holy See delegation.

August 1975 FAO issues 'Ceres' medal, bearing on one side the image of Mother Teresa as sculpted by British artist Michael Rizzelo. The obverse pictures an undernourished child about to be embraced by two outstretched arms.

7 October 1975 Silver Jubilee of the founding of the Order of the Mothers of Charity.

23 October 1975 Mother Teresa received the first Albert Schweitzer International Prize.

24 October 1975 To UN Headquarters to speak at the Temple of Understanding Conference.

25 October 1975 Attended a meeting of the UN Association of the USA in Washington.

2 November 1975 Awarded an honorary Doctorate of Laws by St Francis Xavier University, Antigonish, Canada.

January 1976 Awarded an honorary Doctorate by the Shantinikitan Vishra Bharat University, India.

8 April 1976 Centre started in Mexico.

26 April 1976 Centre started in Guatemala to care for those rendered homeless by the earthquake of 4 February 1976.

13 June 1976 Contemplative Branch of the Mothers of Charity 'Sisters of the Word' founded in New York, USA.

15–17 August 1976 Second meeting of the International Association of Co-Workers of Mother Teresa in Lippstadt, Germany.

10 June 1977   Prince Philip, Chancellor of Cambridge University, England, bestowed an honorary degree of Doctor of Divinity on Mother Teresa.

1977   Houses of Sisters opened in Manila and Haiti, and of Brothers in Hong Kong and Korea. 'Brothers of the Word' Contemplative Brothers opened in Rome.